Rebuilding the Ruins

Rebuilding the Ruins

Following God's call to serve Syria

SAMARA LEVY

HODDER &
STOUGHTON

...ghton

The right of Samara Levy to be identified as the Author of the Work has been asserted by her in accordance with the Copyright, Designs and Patents Act 1988.

Unless indicated otherwise, Scripture quotations are taken from the *Holy Bible, New International Version* (Anglicised edition). Copyright © 1979, 1984, 2011 by Biblica Inc.® Used by permission. All rights reserved.

Scripture quotations marked ESV are taken from *The Holy Bible, English Standard Version®*, copyright 2001 by Crossway, a publishing ministry of Good News Publishers. Used by permission. All rights reserved.

Scripture quotations marked NLT are taken from *The Holy Bible, New Living Translation*, copyright © 1996, 2004, 2015 by Tyndale House Foundation. Used by permission of Tyndale House Publishers, Inc. All rights reserved.

A CIP catalogue record for this title is available from the British Library

Hardback ISBN 978 1 529 39077 3
eBook ISBN 978 1 529 39079 7

Typeset in Bembo MT by Palimpsest Book Production Ltd, Falkirk, Stirlingshire

Printed and bound in Great Britain by Clays Ltd, Elcograf S.p.A.

Hodder & Stoughton policy is to use papers that are natural, renewable and recyclable products and made from wood grown in sustainable forests. The logging and manufacturing processes are expected to conform to the environmental regulations of the country of origin.

Hodder & Stoughton Ltd
Carmelite House
50 Victoria Embankment
London EC4Y 0DZ

www.hodderfaith.com

To my Family.

*To my wonderful husband, for your patience,
support and time, enabling me to pour so much
of my heart into this work.*

*To my precious children, for sharing me, and my time,
with the children of Syria.*

*To my selfless parents, for the unconditional love,
encouragement and support you have given me
over the years.*

*To my Syrian brothers and sisters, for sharing your heart
with me.*

They will rebuild the ancient ruins
    and restore the places long devastated;
they will renew the ruined cities
    that have been devastated for generations.

Isaiah 61:4

Contents

Foreword

One Sunday several years ago, after the morning service at St Peter's, a young woman waited to speak to me. I knew her name but barely anything about her. She began to talk rapidly about Syrian refugees and how we must do something to help. I confess that when people approach me with 'ideas for the church to do', I generally listen as politely and for as long as I am able, and then push back, suggesting that *they* are the church, so why don't *they* do something? However, as I prepared to give my stock response, I began to realise this was different. It was obvious from the conviction and clarity of this woman that helping the refugees was something she was absolutely going to do, whether we, her church, joined in or not – and I was not being begged for help in getting her plan off the ground, but rather, I was being given an opportunity to be part of a great adventure. And it wasn't difficult to agree to her small ask: simply encouraging church members to bring along their unwanted warm winter clothing one Sunday, to be collected and sent out to a refugee camp.

What has happened in the five years since that conversation is extraordinary – and *Rebuilding the Ruins* is the story. I have watched it all unfold, marvelling and often pinching myself that it is really happening. Samara tells how God has led her from collecting a few bin liners full of clothes in her back bedroom at home, to launching an appeal for a multi-million-pound hospital in Syria. The book is an adventure story, a tale of daring to do, chronicling events, but also bringing to life particular turning points and incidents along the way, through carefully remembered interactions and details.

However, this book is about more than an adventure, and I found myself reading it not merely as an interested or fascinated third-party observer. It is interesting and exciting, yes, but it is also personally challenging and hugely encouraging in relating how calling happens in our lives. This is why I commend it to everyone to read, not because we will all feel as passionate about this particular cause, but because Samara's story tells us how God can use each and every one of us, whatever the cause and whatever the passion he gives us. It is a cliché because it is true: God uses ordinary people to do extraordinary things. And Samara is an exemplar.

God spoke to me in various ways through *Rebuilding the Ruins*. First, the book clarifies that availability, not ability, is the key characteristic required in anyone wishing to find and follow a God-directed vision. Samara is a stay-at-home mother with a nursing background, living in Sussex. She had no prior experience of Syria, of the Middle East, of fundraising, of logistics and operations, of vision-casting or of team-building. But she felt a nudge from God to do something, and she said, 'Yes.' Second, it shows that big things have small beginnings. Samara could never have imagined what would happen in such a short amount of time, but she trusted God and was inspired herself by the stories of how God used others, and simply took the first step, and then the one after that, and so on. Third, it illuminates the fact that God is the God of miracles. All things are possible. Time and again the book recounts occasions when God makes a way where there is no way. This is the most uplifting story of how God interweaves individuals and histories and 'chance' encounters for the purposes of his kingdom. Finally, it offers proof that God-directed dreams require our hard work. For as much as God has so clearly orchestrated doors opening, funds arriving and logistics clicking into place, he has done so through Samara's passion, persistence, ability to overcome disappointment and discouragement, tenacity, and personal sacrifice.

These are just four things I picked up from this book for my own life, and you will probably find others for yours. God has used Samara's story to help change the way I want to live my own life: bigger, braver, more trusting – and more extraordinary. Thank you, Samara!

Archie Coates
Vicar, St Peter's, Brighton – July 2019

Introduction

It is a gift to be given each day, one at a time, with little insight into the future. If we knew what lay ahead of us in our journey through life, many of us might not have the courage to set out in the first place. Had someone shown me five years ago the goals I am now dreaming of, the nature and number of challenges I have faced along the way, or the things I would see, hear and experience, I might have been too terrified to take the first step of faith, or each subsequent one. In my case, ignorance has been bliss.

The Syrian war has been one of the most complicated conflicts of our generation, and the politics are more multifaceted than they seem. My aim is to be neutral, and I have tried very hard to steer clear of the politics and controversies related to this war, without being unfaithful to the lives I have encountered in Syria. Discussions about chemical attacks or about who is right or wrong serve only to distract from the most burning question in my heart: how do we best help these people who in a few years have lived and endured more than anyone should have to witness in a lifetime?

My focus instead has been simply on telling my story and retelling the stories of a handful of the many ordinary people I have met during my times in Syria. These are the simple people who have lost everything, and who have no hidden agenda in telling me their stories. These people have told me what they lived, experienced and suffered during this war. Many of their stories have been a torrent of grief, pain and loss.

I have had the privilege of visiting this beautiful country a number of times during the course of the conflict. I have visited well over one hundred displaced families existing in makeshift living spaces across the country. I have travelled across Syria to numerous cities and some rural areas. I have also spent time in places that had previously been held under siege for a number of years, including east Aleppo, parts of Ghouta near Damascus, Hamadiyah in Homs and Deir ez-Zor.

Visiting these places and talking with the people who lived there before, during and after the sieges has been an eye-opener, and has given me a very different perspective on the war in Syria than it would have been possible to have gained from the UK.

Additionally, I have had the chance to visit a handful of orphanages and schools and also a number of hospitals, both public and private, as well as a few churches.

Given the extremely complex situation that still exists in Syria, and the dangers people have been exposed to since 2011, I have used pseudonyms for each of the people I encountered in Syria, as well as for those in our team, and most of the small field hospitals we have provided. I have also changed details in some of the stories I have told about individuals, and in some instances I have not revealed the locations of certain projects. This is to protect the people, their privacy, their families and our work, by not making them obviously identifiable. There are still terrorist and armed factions on the ground, and there are also many corrupt and criminal groups attracted by the potentially lucrative prospect of foreign aid.

Throughout the book there are references to passages in the Bible that have been important in directing parts of my journey. A handful of different translations have been used, including the English Standard Version, the New Living Translation and the New International Version, depending on what was to hand at the time.

It is my heartfelt prayer that as you read this book you will be challenged and shaken, as well as encouraged and inspired. Most of all, it is my prayer that you will do many more amazing things than these in your journey in faith, and that you will begin by picking up a stone, helping us to put it in place and start rebuilding the ruins.

I

Damascus

The Early Hours of 10 May 2018

My heart thumped as I sat rigidly on the barely used bedcovers. Sleep was out of the question now. At least the first explosions I heard after waking from my short-lived slumber were distant, lending a vague sense of security to my situation.

Memories flooded back of unnerving nights a year before in Aleppo, Syria's second-largest city. As I had lain in the sleeping bag with my eyes wide open, the noise of detonated bombs cut through the darkness. I had been reassured by the seeming lack of alarm on the part of my hosts, who neither blinked nor modulated the pitch of their voices with each explosion. These war sounds had been alien to my experience of life, but I had studied these people's faces and responses at each of the unfamiliar noises. They were unconcerned by far-off booms, or even by the closer sounds of machine guns piercing the air. Having lived through the worst of the fighting in Aleppo, they, like everyone else in their city, had become accustomed to this background cacophony of conflict.

Tonight, however, I was alone in my hotel room in Damascus. The darkness served only to intensify the silence, which, by contrast, magnified the explosions bursting in on the stillness of the night. There were no hosts to reassure me this time. The insistence of these increasingly loud explosions tore away any reassurances I had at first given myself that these bombs were in the distance, so would not be a threat.

Suddenly a massive blast thundered outside my window, lighting up the room. My whole body jumped at the unexpected, ear-splitting proximity of the explosion. I broke out in a cold sweat, while adrenalin pumped through my veins. My heart was pounding. This one had been too close. A multitude of thoughts flooded my mind as I tried to process the reality of what was going on around me. What would become of my children and husband back in the UK if anything happened to me?

The phone buzzed softly as I called Dr A, our director in Syria. I was grateful at this late hour that he did not possess a great appetite for sleep. He answered quickly, already aware of the attack through my stream of increasingly anxious messages.

'Is this normal here?' I enquired in the typically English way of not wanting to make a fuss. My body and mind did not feel as calm as my voice may have sounded.

'No,' he replied. 'Israel is attacking Damascus. No one is sleeping in the city now.'

Since the siege of east Ghouta had been broken, the most obvious ongoing disturbance in the region of Damascus was the fighting around Yarmouk. Shells and rockets were persistently fired from this last remaining area around Damascus controlled by jihadists while the Syrian army focused its attacks on breaking the siege there. On the one hand, I should be relieved if this attack was not from ISIS, or another jihadist army attacking this area, as these groups specifically target civilians. A western Christian would be perfect prey for them, and an ideal candidate for a ransom if kidnapped. On the other hand, if Israel was attacking, they would be using bigger and more expensive rockets with a greater range of height, distance and destruction, and with no guarantee of where they would hit.

The sinking sensation in the pit of my stomach grew, especially as I had asked for a room on the tenth floor. It hadn't been our intention for me to stay there that night, but the shelling we had narrowly missed in the city the previous afternoon had persuaded us to look for a hotel a couple of kilometres outside the centre.

While Haitham was driving us through Damascus that day, I had heard the sound of an explosion echo through the streets. Shortly afterwards, we saw on local and social media that it had killed and wounded a number of civilians. The shell, believed to have been fired from Yarmouk, had hit the same road we had driven through just minutes before. When we drove back through the area a couple of hours later it was hard to see anything had happened there. The Syrians have developed an uncanny ability during this war to dust themselves off, tidy away the debris and carry on with life as if nothing had happened. But it had been a very close escape for us – though I didn't fully register exactly how close until I heard more of these shells hitting areas around us that afternoon while going to visit a widow and her children.

When we pulled up outside the hotel that night, the sight of its tower inspired me with the optimistic notion of looking out over the city of Damascus. Millennia of history and biblical significance were spread across this ancient and bustling city alongside its chaotic traffic and the continuous noise of horns beeping. It was on the road to this city that St Paul had met with Jesus and had been converted from an aggressive oppressor of early Christians to one of the most faithful and courageous evangelical Christians who ever lived. It was in Damascus that he preached the gospel for the first time. The opportunity to drink in the atmosphere of this city and its starry backdrop from a high vantage point seemed too good to miss.

But now, in the middle of this heavy and terrifying rocket attack, I drew my knees closer to my chest in an effort to feel less vulnerable and exposed. My view and my mood were now cruelly at odds with any romantic idea I might have had of soaking in the beauty of Syria's capital city by night.

'There is an orange light flying through the sky,' I told Dr A in an alarmed voice, as my eyes fixed on it through the window. 'I think it is going past. No. Wait … it is coming this way!'

'Really?' Dr A replied, trying to make sense of my anxious attempts to describe what I was seeing.

'I can't stay here if it's coming this way!' I had by now lost the composure I had tried to convey at the start of the conversation. I ran past the bed to the windowless bathroom that was closer to the centre of the building.

Later, Dr A gently explained to me that the bathroom wouldn't have offered any protection. One of those rockets would have blasted straight through all the walls. Like everyone else faced with this unimaginably frightening situation, including all the Syrian people who have lived through similar attacks, I had panicked, desperately attempting to take some kind of charge over a situation far beyond my control. The feeling of being so unsafe and helpless is hard to accurately convey to anyone who hasn't lived it.

I waited for a minute or so for the prolonged silence to be broken, and it seemed strange when it continued. I ventured out of the bathroom to look tentatively out of the window. Another orange light, like a sinister firework, travelled slowly across the sky. In mid-air the light grew dim, then disappeared.

'Are they anti-missile defences?' I asked Dr A. 'They seem to be burning out in the middle of the sky.'

'I expect so. The army will be intercepting the rockets.' Dr A's voice was slow and methodical. Having lived through more than seven years of this ruthless conflict in some of the worst areas, he was now an expert.

'What are these other sounds? I can't see them, but I can hear loud noises like a jet flying overhead. Are they rockets?'

'They could be,' he said, sounding calmer than I felt.

There was a hill to the left of my window view, not more than a few kilometres away. Some of the anti-missile defences seemed to be coming from there, and there were explosions around it. More explosions happened in the sky as anti-missile defences hit the rockets. Others I could only hear, while still more occurred close enough to where I was that the flashes lit up the darkness around the hotel, the deafening booms shaking my body.

Every thundering blast turned my stomach, and I spent much of the night shaking. I learnt what people mean when they talk of being paralysed by fear. The tightness in my chest lasted most of the night as I ran through the different scenarios in my head. Nothing I could tell myself lessened the unease I felt. I wanted desperately to be anywhere else. I thought about leaving there and then, in the middle of the night, before realising I might be less safe outside than I was staying in my room. Perhaps the checkpoints would not allow anyone to pass and I would end up stranded in an unfamiliar street in the middle of a war zone.

As I sat in the dark making plans to leave the city as soon as it was safe to do so, I was struck by the sheer injustice of the situation for the Syrian people. I had come of my own free will and could leave as soon as there was an opportunity. I had the luxury of going back to my safe life in England to recover from this life-changing ordeal, but this was not an option for the people here. These people had homes, jobs and families here; this was their country, and these were their lives.

Damascus was already the new home to huge numbers of displaced people who had fled the fighting and the attacks, during which jihadist armies took the villages and suburbs surrounding this city and others which had previously been their homes. Many had nowhere else to go. Even if they did have, how would they find work to support their families, given the depleted economy of Syria, a country on its knees? Many people were already living hand to mouth in Damascus and could not now afford the cost of travelling to another destination.

It occurred to me as I sat in the dark that night that if my hotel was hit I might need to run quickly. I immediately switched on the lamp to get dressed and packed my wheel-along hand-luggage case. If I had to run, however, this bag would slow me down. My passport and most precious items were stowed in my small rucksack which, in the worst case, I could take with me, leaving the hand luggage behind. After labouring over the decision about whether I should try to leave, I wondered how anyone with small children took such a tough decision. To run through something so horrifying on your own would be terrifying, but to be forced to take a life-threatening risk like this with children or a baby was inconceivable. Yet this had been the reality for innumerable Syrian people during this cruel conflict.

Previously, I had tried to imagine the kind of events that would force someone to leave their home with nothing. Many of the displaced people we had served had fled from their homes with only the clothes they were wearing, or just their pyjamas, and had not even stopped to gather their identification documents. In the early days, I had wondered how such a scenario could come about: surely it didn't take long to pick up your papers? But no amount of imagining or empathising can give you any realistic idea of the absolute terror brought on by every shattering explosion close by. A rocket hitting your building, or your neighbours' building, would be enough to send you running in terror, without a thought for anything except survival. That night in the hotel gave me a tiny taste of what life has been like for so many Syrians – just a small taste – but also the understanding that listening to someone else describe the fear can in no way prepare anyone for the reality of how they will feel or respond, psychologically or physically, to the stress of an event like this.

In the early hours, Dr A and I exchanged messages, and I was able to draw just a little reassurance from his extensive experience of this war and his calm response to this attack. One of his relatives lived very near an area in Damascus where some of these rockets were hitting. He, his wife and young children were sheltering underground that night. A house in their area was hit by one of the rockets, killing the family inside. Dr A told me the next day that he had spent the night on the phone speaking with various people who might know more about the situation to try to understand the threat, and how to get us out at the first opportunity.

As the sun began to rise and the birds started to sing again, the war sounds subsided. I knelt by the side of my bed, praying. I remembered a promise made to me the year before. It was this promise that gave me, an ordinary stay-at-home mother of two young children in the UK, the confidence and assurance to make this and each of the other trips I have made to Syria – perhaps the most dangerous war zone in the world.

2

The Promise

February to March 2017

Having taken more than a year to make the decision to visit Syria, I was beginning to feel uneasy. I was sitting on the floor one Saturday with my children, aged seven and four, and we were playing with Lego. It was just two weeks after I had made the commitment to go, and my youngest son wrapped his arms around my neck, showering me with kisses.

'You are the bestest, most precious mummy in the whole world. I love you so much!' he beamed, planting a wet kiss on my cheek. I felt as though my heart skipped a beat at his innocent, trusting words. What if something bad happened to me? What would become of my children? I pulled him closer, softly kissing the top of his head. I looked over at my eldest son building a racing car from plastic blocks and wheels and felt a strong urge to pull him onto my lap too, and hold him tightly.

My rational side argued that I had every reason to feel concerned. The statistics published by official bodies for the previous year demonstrated that Syria towered above every country in the world for the staggeringly high number of kidnappings and killings of humanitarian workers; astoundingly, in the same year, two thirds of all the reported global attacks against healthcare professionals and facilities took place in Syria. Given that our work was focused on providing medical help as well as humanitarian aid in Syria, this began to play on my mind.

My decision to visit this war-torn country had not been made lightly. I had spent a long time thinking and praying about it, as well as talking to contacts running other charities. Their comments were always the same: 'You don't need to go, Samara. You are a mother. People will understand if you don't.'

But no matter how sympathetic about my situation our supporters might be, I could not come to terms with not seeing, hearing, smelling and tasting the world I spent such a huge proportion of my time serving and interacting with. My heart was for the people in Syria, and I was talking with our teams there daily. I wanted to reach out and touch the lives of the people we were supporting. I wanted to look into their eyes, to stand with them, to hold their hands and show them they are loved. As much as it might be easier and safer, I could not do it with authenticity exclusively from the UK. A trip to Syria was problematic on every level, but I felt a burden on my heart telling me to go. I had tried to push the thought away over the previous year, but it kept returning and I couldn't shake it off. Finally, I put the matter in God's hands. Although I had prayed about it before, there was something different in my heart as I prayed this time. I told God that I felt I was meant to go, but that I didn't feel I could rely on my feelings. It needed to come from him. I told God I was willing to give my life serving him, but I didn't want to leave my children without a mother unless it was his will. I prayed that if it was his wish for me to go, and that even if I died there, I would be ready. But I didn't want to risk my life unnecessarily on a whim – I needed to be sure it was his plan. I told him I was waiting for him to tell me to go before I started making any plans.

A few weeks after this prayer, I heard his instruction clearly. I had been sent some pictures from an orphanage in Aleppo. Four or five sets of bunk beds and eight to ten children were crammed into each small room. Clothes hung off the ends of the bunks as there was nowhere else to store them. The windows had no glass, and the rooms had no heating. That winter had been one of the harshest anyone in Syria remembered, with sub-zero temperatures and even snow in many places. Yet this was one of the best and most well-catered-for orphanages in the area, and there were so many other orphans in more deprived settings.

My eyes rested on the pictures of these haunted, shell-shocked little faces. Their pain-filled eyes, which had seen and lived through every child's worst nightmare, were windows into their souls. Tears blurred my vision as something stirred in my heart, the heart of a mother. These beautiful children had been precious to their parents just as mine are to me, but those parents' lives had been mercilessly torn from them. They had no choice in leaving their children to fend for themselves in this cruel and barren world. Most importantly, I thought as I wiped the tears from my eyes, these children are precious to God.

'Go to them.' His voice spoke clearly and firmly to my heart. It was a direct yet gentle instruction, the 'still, small voice of calm' as described in the old-fashioned hymn we used to sing at school. I was going to Syria. It was settled.

The most important thing I needed to do before I could commit and book the ticket was to talk with my husband. Two years before, I had broached the subject of travelling to Iraq. His vehemently negative response at the time had left no question about his feelings. I'm sure most caring husbands and fathers would have responded with similar fervour. After discussing the situation with my vicar, I followed his advice not to pursue the idea at the time if it made my husband so uncomfortable.

Two years later, however, the nature of and extent of our work had grown significantly, and I had greater commitments which carried more substantial responsibilities. We were now establishing small field hospitals and medical teams to serve in the midst of the crisis. I felt a weightier calling to support some of the orphans and widows left in the wake of this cruel war which had stolen the lives of so many parents.

I prayed for God to move my husband's heart. I could not expect him to welcome the idea or embrace it with open arms, but I asked God to give him some level of acceptance about what I needed to do. I didn't want any resentment or bad feelings lingering over our family.

'My feelings haven't changed since we last spoke about this,' came his response. We then talked about many things, and I pointed out what privileged lives we were leading, and how our children had everything they wanted and needed – most importantly, a mother and father. What if one or both of us were killed and our children were left to fend for themselves in a country brought to its knees by poverty and war? Wouldn't we want someone somewhere in this world to be willing to put their neck on the line to help our precious children? Surely our children would be worth that?

Events and circumstances in this world only change when individuals are willing to take risks and walk the extra mile for someone else. This is the true meaning of sacrificial giving: to give for the benefit of someone else, to the point of our own discomfort. In our comfortable lives in the West, we have fewer practical illustrations of real sacrifice because so much is provided for us; in the UK, for example, we have, among other things, a welfare infrastructure, social services provision for neglected or orphaned children, as well for those who are elderly or otherwise vulnerable, an amazing national health service, an excellent education system, and food banks.

My husband listened in silence.

'I don't want you to go, and would prefer that you didn't,' he eventually responded. 'But I understand why it is important to you. I understand why it is important that you go.'

As I thanked God for this shift in my husband's heart, I also thanked him for the fact that he cared enough about my safety and our family to try to persuade me against going to one of the most dangerous places on earth.

Two weeks later, the planning was under way. I had not yet told anyone else about the trip, feeling it safer not to publicise it. But my initial positive mindset began to be replaced by feelings of apprehension for my children. That Sunday I couldn't shake the nervous, churning feeling in my stomach as I walked into church. Throughout the service, the feeling nagged at me. At the end, when our vicar gave an opportunity for people to receive prayer, I was one of the first in the queue. I stood at the front with my eyes closed, then felt a hand rest lightly on my shoulder. I kept my eyes closed as I heard an unfamiliar voice praying. I didn't say a word to the lady who was speaking, she simply prayed for me. After a little while she stopped and said: 'I feel God is saying to you, "Yes, it is a dangerous place, but I will protect you, and I will protect the team. It's not safe, but I am safe."' I opened my eyes and stared at her through my tears. I recognised this lady, but we had never spoken before. She didn't know anything of my plans to go to Syria. I had kept them secret. She had spoken a promise which came directly from God. The realisation that God had spoken to me so directly about the issue pressing my heart, through a woman who knew nothing about my plans, felt overwhelming.

'Do you know how significant your words are right now?' I replied, wiping the tears from my cheeks. 'I am planning on going to Syria, but over the last couple of days I have been feeling very anxious about it. God knew exactly what was in my heart and has told me exactly what I needed to hear.'

'I felt him saying he is going to send you to Syria, but I didn't dare say it,' she replied immediately. I couldn't blame her for holding back. It is not a statement anyone would want to get wrong or make lightly to a mother of two young children. It was a deeply moving and emotional experience which I will never forget. There was now no doubt in my heart that God was in control of this trip, and I knew that whatever happened while I was in Syria, he would protect us, as long as we were listening and responsive to him and working within his will. Nothing would happen to me unless it was part of God's plan. As he had said to me so clearly, there is no safer place than being in God's will.

Some of the practicalities of this trip had also been on my mind. One thing I felt strongly about concerned how we used money raised through our charity. Before I started this work, I had become a little disillusioned with the way many charities work. I felt at this time that everything we raised should go to the cause we raised it for. Since responding to this call, I had worked hard to maintain our ethos of, where possible, not spending money on UK overheads, salaries and expenses. Each warehouse and storage hub we used was given to us free of charge. We had not paid a salary to anyone here in the UK, including me, and almost all of the money we raised, including gift aid, went to transporting our containers of aid to the Middle East, to distributing it as well as other aid bought locally, and to supporting our life-saving medical projects. At times, this placed a greater burden on me and some of our volunteers, but I confess that in this matter I had been obstinately uncompromising at times, perhaps to the occasional frustration of those around me. At times, people remarked that I would not be able to maintain this stance as a registered charity in the long term. They were probably right, but I was not ready to concede anything at this point. Our work is about love in action, and of service, and I am always keen to draw on people's skills and experience, given in love, before paying a professional. Some of the charities I have encountered have achieved marvellous things and built pivotal relationships through travelling and spending time with the people and projects they support abroad. This is an essential aspect of working in international locations. But I have seen others who appear to send their staff abroad without a clear vision or any return for the charity money they put into these trips. I have also become more aware of the existence of a strange kind of poverty tourism. While I can see the rationale behind taking supporters to see the reality of life in the areas they wish to raise support for, I have also been acutely conscious that these vulnerable lives we are looking into need to be treated with dignity and respect.

Often these people who are poor and needy may feel an obligation to be polite to foreign visitors, or perhaps they hope for help from these visits – help that never materialises. I recall the words of someone working with another charity who sounded so excited about a visit she was about to make as she told me she had never visited a refugee camp before. Something about it didn't sit right in my heart. Visiting refugee camps is not exciting, and I could not go simply for the sake of ticking off an experience. On each visit I have made, I have felt uncomfortable walking into the humble tents, rooms and other living spaces of these unfortunate people, and have found it very hard to take photos of these families or their dwellings. It feels enormously invasive and insensitive, and I try to avoid it as much as possible, even though I know we also need to show our work, and the reality of the situation, to our supporters.

Often, well-meaning actions that we might envisage, from the comfort of our different life experiences here in the West, as being encouraging or beneficial may be received very differently or even have negative repercussions. We have to be so careful and sensitive when working in such a complex place and in communities that are so riddled with poverty. I didn't want to adopt the attitude of going just for the sake of going, and in doing so spending valuable resources which could have been used to benefit the people we are ultimately trying to help. But it had been more than two and a half years since I had sent my first consignment of aid to Iraq, with so much having subsequently been achieved on the ground without me even having set foot in the Middle East. By this time, going there had become an absolute necessity.

Since I started this work, I have been able to devote my time and energy to it as my husband generously supported our family. Our domestic housekeeping budget had covered most of my UK travel and phone expenses, but there were occasions when extra expenses needed to be covered, and this had been a little awkward. I had set up an account for my personal expenses, separate from our charity account, with an organisation that processes donations for people working in Christian ministry. I put a link on our giving page beneath the other charity-giving options, but didn't imagine anyone would notice it, and wondered how I would find the money to cover this trip. Again, I decided to put it in God's hands. I prayed, saying that I preferred not to use any of this charity money to cover this trip, and went as far as stating that I didn't even want to ask anyone to help cover these expenses. I asked God to provide this money without me having to ask anyone except him.

Over these last few years, having seen God provide for this work over and over again, in situations where I had no ability to fulfil specific needs, I have learnt so much about stepping back and trusting him to provide rather than trying myself to provide when I can't. God calls us to rely on him in our weakness so that he can give more than we could ever achieve through our own ability.

About ten days later, I got an email through from the donation-processing organisation that I had used to set up my personal account; they said they were about to transfer £1,100 to me. I was amazed! How had that happened so quickly? Most of that money, it turned out, had been donated by a beautiful and compassionate mother who had been supporting our work in various ways, but with whom I had not had any recent contact. A week or so later we talked as I wanted to thank her. She asked me how much more money I needed. I did not know. She told me that a couple of days before, the Holy Spirit had asked her to cover the rest of the costs for the trip. So in the space of a few weeks, I had moved from my well-rehearsed stance of saying no every time someone asked if I had been to Syria or had plans to go there, to having a clear command, followed by a promise, and then also sufficient funds provided to carry out my first trip. There could be no question about it: this was God's plan.

One of the characteristics of God I have become more aware of is that he doesn't always choose the people others would choose to do his work. He looks beyond our skills, our experience, or anything in our outward appearance which others would judge us by. Instead, he looks straight into our hearts. He often uses the most unlikely candidates to be his hands, feet and voice – the likes of Moses, David, Gideon, Amos, Peter, Paul and John the Baptist. Even Jesus was not the image others would have chosen as the Messiah. In some instances, those prophets would not have chosen themselves either. But God's way is different from ours.

If anyone had been looking around my big church in Brighton for the ideal candidate to do this work, I feel sure they wouldn't have chosen me. I wouldn't have chosen myself. There are many more qualified, more experienced, more socially skilled and better-connected people than me. I was a stay-at-home mum who didn't appear on the outside to have much to offer at that point in my life. I didn't have a degree in international development, nor any experience in charity work at that time. I had not done any big fundraising projects before and I didn't have a large network of contacts. Most importantly, if anyone had been looking for someone to start a charity serving the troubled Middle East, someone to spend time in one of the most dangerous war zones in the world, who in their right mind would choose a mother of two young children? Only God would make a choice like this!

As I planned the trip, I thought of the challenges and restrictions that went hand in hand with a mother leaving her children for a short time in order to visit Syria. I felt that my position as a mother imposed limitations on the amount of time I could go for and on what I could achieve in this short time. I wondered why God hadn't chosen someone who had more time for travelling, or who could even go and live in a place like Syria. But as I spent time in that troubled land and focused more attention on who we hoped to support, and how, I felt more convinced that God had deliberately chosen a mother to be responsible for this work. He wanted someone who would see, understand and anticipate, without being told, what a poor widow needs for herself and her children, and who would love and respond to the needs that were apparent in these broken lives and communities.

3

A Mother's Calling

2013–14

'Wow, sweetheart! How did you manage that?' I gasped, as something brown and ominous seeped out of the bottom of my toddler's trouser leg. I had begun to make the connection with feeding him grapes, though I was never able to fathom how they could go through him at such high speed, or with such dramatic results. Dealing with these consequences quickly, in the right place, was essential for damage limitation and to mini-mise overall disruption to the day. Swiftly I carried him to the bathroom, where I could depend on a wipe-clean floor and the close proximity of the bath. I mentally ran through the precise operation that would now be needed to ensure that I could redirect my attention as soon as possible to the dinner I had left cooking. I was grateful that the outflow from his nappy had only travelled downwards into his trousers, that I peeled off, and not upwards as well, to cover his T-shirt and jumper in addition to his bottoms and socks. By now, the evidence had escaped onto the bathroom floor, onto which I discarded his soiled trousers. I whispered my gratitude that nothing had oozed out onto the carpet on the way to the bathroom. Placing my reeking toddler into the empty bath, I held the shower head away from him while I waited for the water to warm enough to shower him down. He giggled and squealed in delight, trying to avoid the jet of warm water as I directed it onto his skin. After cleaning the floor, drying my son and then applying a new nappy, I redressed him. Putting the stinking clothes directly into the washing machine, and the offending nappy straight into the outdoor bin, I breathed a sigh of relief before realising that the pasta was overdone.

As I strained the soggy fusilli swirls through the colander, my thoughts drifted back to the reports I had heard earlier that day. I was still struggling to process the news that there were Syrian families living in camps in the snow. This itself was hard to imagine, but it was beyond difficult to believe that any of them, especially those little children, could be wearing flip-flops in the snow. How could this be possible? When I talked with my mother, she said that she too had heard these reports. These people had fled from their homes in the summer with only the clothes on their backs. But six months later, those clothes were wholly inappropriate for the change in season. Having lost everything they ever owned, they were now living in harsh camp conditions with little or nothing. How could any mother raise her children in this way?

How would a mother living in a tent in the snow deal with a leaking nappy like the one I had just dealt with? How would she cope with the day-to-day wetting and soiling if she didn't have nappies in the first place? How would she deal with the terrible nappy rash that would be inevitable if she seldom managed to get hold of nappies and was rarely able to change them? How would she wash her faeces-covered child if she only had freezing-cold water, or perhaps no water at all? What would she do with a fifteen-month-old toddler like mine who had just started walking, when she had no shoes to put on his feet? How would or could she keep him confined to a small and bitterly cold tent in winter when the only alternative would be to let him walk outside in the snow, or freezing mud with no shoes? My mind was racing, and my heart was struggling to keep up. It was too much to process.

In the comfort of our centrally heated, double-glazed home, with hot water, washing machines, and all the clothes we needed, and where we were struggling to lose weight rather than to buy enough food, motherhood had presented many challenges for me over the last four years. As beautiful and rewarding as it was, it was also exhausting, and it pushed me to my limit in so many ways. So how did a mother in that appalling situation in Syria get out of bed in the morning, knowing how tough the day ahead of her would be? How did these women continue to keep putting one foot in front of the other and avoid sinking into the deepest depression after everything they had lost, and with each of the challenges they faced every day, just trying to keep their children warm, fed and healthy? What kind of hope could they have for the future?

I shuddered as I thought of these women and their children. I looked at the pile of beautiful clothes my youngest child had outgrown, and which I had been saving for my sister's baby, due in a few months. Two passages from the Bible came to mind: 'Anyone who has two shirts should share with the one who has none' (Luke 3:11) and, 'I was naked, and you gave me clothing' (Matt. 25:36 NLT). It was very simple. We had plenty; these people did not. We had more than one; they had none. I felt that my mandate to share what I had was straightforward, but the means of doing so was less apparent. How could I find one of these camps in Syria and send our clothes to it? This weighed heavily on my heart over the next few days. I could not stop thinking about these people. I desperately wanted to share our clothes with them but had no idea how to start. I asked God. A day or two later my mother showed me a blanket she had been knitting to send out to the Syrian refugees.

'Where are you sending them?' I asked, wide-eyed. 'I have so much to send.' I packaged everything up and posted the parcels to the address I had been given. It seemed a time-consuming and expensive way of sending these items as each package had to weigh under two kilograms and took time to weigh, wrap and address, then each cost nearly £15 to post. I was so grateful and relieved for the opportunity to send these things, but after wrapping the fourteenth or fifteenth package, I felt there must be a more efficient and cost-effective way of doing this. The comparatively luxurious lifestyle we live in the UK kept playing on my mind. I wanted to collect clothes at my son's school – warm, good-quality clothes our children don't need – and send them to those children who had nothing.

I asked the organisation I sent our clothes to whether I could try to fill a lorry and send it to them. 'No' was the answer, as the taxes would be unmanageable. Disappointed, I wondered how else I could try to organise something like this. Every charity I contacted politely turned down the idea of sending a used-clothing collection to Syria or the surrounding areas. I couldn't shake off the feeling of frustration I had, knowing how many good-quality, unneeded clothes were in many homes around the UK. Frustrated that it didn't seem possible to organise a lorry full of winter clothes and shoes to send to these brothers and sisters of ours, I prayed, asking God to show me what I had to do to make something like this happen. He simply said, 'Start collecting.'

I was not impressed. This wasn't the way I liked to work. I wanted to know how everything would come together, who would do what, how it would happen and where it would go before I started. So instead, I carried on with my life, feeling disheartened.

A couple of months later, the idea came back to me very suddenly after reading *God's Smuggler*, by Brother Andrew, which talked about refugees living in camps. (I should point out here that I have never smuggled any of our aid into the Middle East!) The idea of sending this aid felt like a big burden I couldn't shake off. I felt a sense of urgency to organise a lorry load of winter clothes and shoes for the people who had lost their homes, and I couldn't ignore this feeling. I started looking into it again and kept drawing blanks. None of the organisations I contacted were interested in helping in any way, even if I offered to do all the work, ensuring that everything was clean, sorted and packed nicely.

In my frustration I again asked God to show me what I had to do to get this organised. For a second time, he simply said, 'Start collecting.'

Reluctantly, I wondered whether I should indeed do just that. I told a couple of mums at school that I wanted to collect winter clothes and shoes to send to the Syrians, and they responded with more enthusiasm than I felt myself, given the obstacles I'd encountered.

After making a few more calls and meeting more closed doors,

I put the couple of bags I had collected into the spare room, then closed the door. I felt disheartened and at a loss as to how to make this happen. Months drifted by, and I would occasionally feel frustrated by seeing the bags when I went into the spare room. Then the summer of 2014 came.

After seeing news of the horrific events that were taking place in northern Iraq and the way whole families were being tortured, slaughtered and driven from their homes when ISIS took their towns and villages, I felt heartbroken. Our Christian brothers and sisters, as well as members of many other communities, were being beheaded, enslaved and driven from their homes along with their little children. They could not take anything with them. For some, in exchange for their lives they sacrificed their homes and every worldly possession they had worked for all their life.

Many left with only the clothes they were wearing, and many lost loved ones. Wives and daughters were raped in front of husbands and fathers, and children as young as three were taken by ISIS. It was too awful to try to imagine what these children or their families were going through.

Through my tears, I prayed for these people. For a few weeks I felt as though I was living through this ordeal with them, as they didn't leave my mind. I read every article I could find detailing what was happening to them. Their suffering weighed so heavily on my heart that I struggled to think about anything else. I prayed for them continuously during this time, and sometimes I would wake in the middle of the night feeling compelled to get on my knees and pray for them.

Many displaced people had fled to the Sinjar Mountains, where they were now dying from sun exposure and dehydration. They were trapped, as ISIS terrorists were waiting for them at the bottom, and so they had nowhere to go, and no food, water or shelter. And it was stiflingly hot in August in the Middle East.

These people had escaped the horror of ISIS only to be confronted by the horror of trying to survive in these harsh conditions, with nothing. I desperately wanted to do something to help them, but what could I do? I was in another country, with two young children and, as a stay-at-home mum, no income.

The last straw was seeing a photograph of a baby who had been beheaded by ISIS. That baby girl was younger than my youngest son. I couldn't believe any human being could do this. At that moment when I was feeling most distraught, I prayed from my heart. I said to God that if there was anything I could do, anything at all that could help, whatever it took, I would do it. I asked him to use me in whichever way he saw fit to help these people. I was spiritually on my knees.

His response surprised me: 'Start collecting.'

Although the issue of clothes had not been on my mind at all during this time, having been given this instruction twice before, I now knew exactly what it meant.

At that moment, I felt God make me a promise, without words, directly to my heart. It is hard to explain, but I felt he gave an assurance to me, in a way that only God can do, giving my heart such certainty without using any words. His assurance was that if I was willing to trust him and step out in faith by starting to collect, without knowing any of the details first, such as where the clothes were going, how they would get there or who was paying, he would provide everything needed. For him to provide, I had first to be willing to step out in faith.

When I took the first little steps towards filling what I didn't realise would be the first of many lorries and containers full of aid, I had no concept at all of where this journey would lead me.

4

Stepping Out of the Boat

August to October 2014

'A whole lorry …' My mother's voice trailed off. Her furrowed brow said what she hadn't. 'Are you sure, Samara?'

I received a large variety of comments over the following weeks and months from well-meaning people. A couple tried to put me off but most were encouraging. I have since learnt that, within the Christian community, and even among some church leaders, there are many who still haven't understood the relationship between stepping out in faith and vulnerability, and God's provision in response to his call. It is something I have learnt much more about over the past five years. Walking God's path rarely involves waiting until everything is planned and provided before taking the plunge; rather, it entails stepping out knowing that he supplies what you need *as you walk*.

From the start of this journey, I have been so thankful to have had the heartfelt support and encouragement of my church, St Peter's, Brighton, and of our vicar, Archie Coates. After I contacted him, pouring out my heart about what I saw happening in Iraq and Syria, and about what I felt we should do to help, he agreed that our church community should respond, and pledged the support of our church.

Over the weeks, months and years that have followed, I have learnt that *having* faith is different from *living* faith. It is one thing to say we have faith in God, that we believe in him and that he can and does work miracles, but this alone is a passive kind of faith. Mature faith is active. If we aren't living out our faith, depending on it, how can we say we have it? Faith not lived is something theoretical. It is like gathering together the various ingredients from a recipe for a cake but then doing nothing with them. You can have the understanding and knowledge of faith, but until you combine those ingredients – and, more importantly, expose them to heat – it will not be cooked and you will not have a cake you can eat. When we personally step out in faith, with the right motivation, we should know for sure that God will use us, working miracles through our own lives.

There was a time in my life when I thought amazing events only happened to other people, or were results to read about in someone else's life. Perhaps they had a different kind of relationship with God. Maybe they had a more direct link to him than I did! Or perhaps they were just more holy than I was. It wasn't that I didn't think he could do something wonderful through me, but I simply didn't have the commitment to selflessly, truly put Jesus first, before my children, husband or anyone else. Nor had I had the courage to be genuinely obedient to his calling, no matter what the cost. There was something in my heart I held back, a little part of me that was afraid and didn't want to leave my comfort zone.

If anyone had told me before all of this that I was not giving Jesus all of myself, I would probably have felt indignant. But there was a little part of me, deep down, which was saying, 'I will do whatever you want Lord, but please don't ask me to do *that*.' Or, 'I am ready to go anywhere, but clearly I can't go *there*.' My desire to serve was there, but it was conditional. I didn't see it that way at the time, but in retrospect, a shift in my attitude was needed before God could use me to do anything more than I was capable of achieving simply through my own ability.

Having read books by some amazingly inspirational and devoted people, such as Jackie Pullinger, Heidi Baker, David Wilkerson and Brother Yun, to name a few, I maintained the view that their situations had been more suitable than mine for serving God. They were younger, or single, or had no children, or had a husband or wife who shared their faith and encouraged their calling, making it possible for them to go to the places they went to and do the things they did. My heart stirred when I read the stories of these people who had been willing to give up everything to serve God among the poorest, most broken. These acts of love were so clearly the heart of Jesus, and they moved my heart too.

How could God possibly use me to do anything as significant as they had done? I was a stay-at-home mum with two small children. My husband has so many wonderful qualities, but he does not share my faith. I felt that I, personally, was lacking, and I didn't have anything to offer. While there are many meaningful ways of serving God, my circumstances felt unfavourable for serving God through working with the poorest communities overseas, in a meaningful way that moved my heart. There were so many excuses and reasons I gave myself to not simply do the things Jesus was calling me to do.

The day this changed was the day my heart broke. It broke when I looked and truly saw the suffering in the Middle East. I am grateful God opened my eyes to let me see a little of what he sees, and to break my heart for what breaks his. I could no longer go on living the life I had been living without doing something. At that moment, I was at a spiritual crossroads, and it was a defining moment in my life. I felt in my heart the significance of my decision over whether to make myself unconditionally available to God or to continue as I had been. I chose to say yes to him.

I put aside my anxieties about what I could or couldn't do, and about my life situation and its lack of suitability. Instead, I surrendered myself completely to God, putting my trust in him. Rather than asking him to help me do something, I asked him instead to use me as he saw fit. It was no longer about what I wanted, or what I thought was good, or what I could or couldn't do, it was now simply about being a servant, ready to do whatever I was asked to do.

When we commit ourselves to doing God's work, to serving him, putting our own desires aside and making his kingdom our priority, he will give us everything we need to do it. It is about submission, willingness to obey, and working for his vision, not for our own.

If you were offered a job by a company and needed certain resources to do the job, your employer would give you what you need to do it – a computer, a phone, stationery, maybe a car, if needed. If you were diligent and made good use of what you had been given, your employer would probably give you more resources, to enable you to do more. If this is what a worldly employer would give, how much more will the master and creator of the universe give us so that we can do his work, serving the poor and serving his kingdom on earth? First, we need to accept the offer and sign the contract, then we need to turn up for work.

We shouldn't expect God to give us lots of things in order that we can begin to serve him; in fact, it is the other way around. He gives us the guidance and infrastructure we need around us to continue the work we have already started for him, with him at the centre. But it is our responsibility to use those resources carefully. We shouldn't expect it to be easy, but we should expect him to be by our side at every step.

People I spoke with embraced the idea of sending a lorry of winter aid to the Middle East, and the clothes started to come in. But they also had questions: 'Where is it going? How will it get there? How can you be sure it goes to the right people?' I didn't have answers. I was, of course, urgently trying to establish these specifics, but it took time and great perseverance. But I was blessed, as many people trusted me and trusted God.

Archie was willing to give some financial support from our church towards the costs of the lorry, and was also willing to ask our church to give clothes, but he needed firm facts, and so did I. The control freak in me was impatient to tick all these boxes and have a firm plan in place. However, I was struggling to find an organisation to partner with in the Middle East. Both Syria and Iraq were in my heart, but I felt that at this point, this aid should be going to Iraq.

Having unsuccessfully emailed around forty non-governmental organisations (NGOs) working in Iraq, I was feeling frustrated. I had practically begged some of the UK charities to put me in touch with the partners they were working with, but none did. I had contacted every person with a connection to Iraq whose details had been passed to me. In those first few weeks I also had spoken a number of times with Paul Reynolds at Mission and Relief Logistics for advice and information, and he was supportive. I had asked him whether he knew of anyone in Iraq, but he didn't. Every door seemed closed.

One afternoon, I stood in my kitchen feeling exasperated. God had assured me he would open all the doors at the right times, yet I felt as though this door had remained firmly shut. In my frustration I said, most ungraciously, 'Lord, you can hear what everyone is saying! I need to tell people where this is going. I have done everything I possibly can to find someone to work with, but I can't do this myself. You promised me you would open all the right doors at the right time! I need you to open the door for me now.'

He simply replied, 'Trust me.'

A little later, I spoke with Paul again and told him I was struggling to find anyone to receive this aid. I confessed that at times I felt like giving up, but I was already in way too deep to be able to. We chuckled about it, and about half an hour later I received an email from Michel Stolk at the head office of Mission and Relief Logistics in the Netherlands. He told me about an NGO in the Kurdistan region of Iraq that they had been sending aid to for ten years through their Dutch office, and offered to put me in touch. This NGO in Iraq partnered with a number of well-known and reputable UK Christian charities, which reassured me. God had kept his part of the bargain, but only after I completely surrendered to him and accepted that I needed *him*, not the other way around.

Some friends and I had planned some fundraisers, and with the contribution from my church, I estimated that we would have around £4,000 of the £6,500 needed for the lorry to take the aid to Iraq, door to door. I had emailed around ten of the bigger churches in Brighton asking them for help, whether with collecting clothes or with funding the lorry. I had not heard back from any of them.

One afternoon the following week, having just got my youngest son off for his daytime nap, I asked God how I could best use this window of time. I felt him tell me to call each of those church leaders I had emailed.

Reluctantly, after being told, one by one, that they were unavailable, I left messages for each of them. Just after I left the last message, the first I had called rang back. He was unenthusiastic about the prospect of collecting clothes at his church. However, my spirits lifted when he said, 'I am the chair of the board of directors for a charity working in the Middle East. We might be able to help you with the extra £2,500 you need to send the lorry.' I was amazed. What were the chances of something like that happening?

He made no promises, other than saying he would take the idea to their trustee meeting the following week. I felt in my heart that this would work – and it had to, because I simply didn't have the capacity by then to think about planning any more fundraisers. I was using every minute of every day just keeping everything moving towards the ultimate goal, alongside looking after my children. I was stretched to my absolute limit.

There had been two sizes of lorry we could use; one carried ninety cubic metres and the other thirty-five. The first was much more cost effective than the second. I remember saying to Archie, 'We serve a big God. I'm sure he would want us to fill the big lorry, not the small one. I think filling the lorry will be easy, the hard bit will be raising the money.' In his kind and encouraging way he had agreed. But I was soon confronted with a new problem. I now realised that, if all went well, we would hopefully soon hit our £6,500 target to pay for the lorry, but finding and storing the ninety cubic metres of clothes was a very different matter. Having measured the rooms in my house many times, I accepted that I needed a bigger storage space to put all the boxes of clothes, shoes and bedding I was appealing for. Many options were suggested to me, but nothing materialised.

When I had first committed to this project, I had no concept of the enormous capacity of these articulated lorries, and I had not been able to envisage the sheer volume of clothing that would be needed to fill one of them. The pressure of finding a storage space big enough to serve this purpose was starting to get to me.

After I had worried about it for a couple of weeks, we prayed about it in our home group led by some good friends who have been a great support. Within thirty-six hours, a self-storage company kindly offered me one of their largest storage units for a couple of weeks. It was a huge relief, and I gratefully transported all the boxes we had sorted and labelled at my house to the unit. When I unloaded those boxes and saw them pushed into the corners of this huge unit, I had a churning feeling in my stomach.

This unit had been measured carefully, and I had calculated that when it was full to nearly two metres high, from front to back and from side to side, I would have enough to fill one of these lorries. When I looked at all the boxes I had brought, I estimated I had somewhere between one and two of the ninety cubic metres these lorries carry! I swallowed hard and started to worry.

It had taken me four weeks to collect this amount, and there were now just two weeks until the deadline I had set for all the clothes to be donated. Seeing the tiny amount I had, and now being aware of the huge amount I needed, I realised I didn't have any chance whatsoever of collecting a further eighty-eight cubic metres of clothes, shoes and bedding in just two weeks! It was impossible. My pitiful attempts over the last four weeks were a painfully clear illustration of this. My heart sank as I started to think about what I would say to Archie and to the director from the charity serving the Middle East, who had both pledged significant sums to pay for a bigger lorry. I knew now that I had no hope of filling even the smaller lorry!

Aside from the shame and embarrassment I felt, there was something bigger weighing on my heart.

Our brothers and sisters who had lost everything needed these things. Winter was fast approaching, and they were going to freeze in the mountains, under bridges and in the car parks where they were sheltering if we didn't fill this lorry. With my youngest son clutched to my hip in one hand and my other hand resting on the small pile of boxes, I prayed the first of many prayers of desperation I would pray over the coming years. I felt weak, small and incapable.

I confessed to God that there was no way I could do this. But I said to him that if he could feed five thousand people with two fish and five loaves of bread, then he could fill this room with the items I had asked for. I asked him to send a flood of clothes, shoes and bedding. I told him I felt mortified by this situation, but asked him not to do it for my sake, but for the sake of our brothers and sisters. They needed these things so desperately. I thanked Jesus in advance for providing everything.

One thing I realised was that I had not yet been to my own wardrobe. I now went to it, literally taking everything I felt I could spare, bearing in mind that these people had lost everything, and winter was coming. I looked at two rain macs hanging there and was again reminded of the passage from Luke 3:11, 'Anyone who has two shirts should share with the one who has none'. One of them was brand new and still had a price tag, and the other was old but in excellent condition. I debated which one I should give. The verse 'Love your neighbour as yourself' (Matt. 22:39) came to mind, so I packed the new one to send to the Middle East.

What happened next was an example of me asking God for a miracle, then trying to make the miracle happen myself! Quite simply, it was impossible for me to fill that lorry in those two weeks, or even in the six weeks I had originally planned. However, in my anxiety, I went home and added many additional things to my original appeal list of clothes, shoes and blankets. I added nappies and sanitary products, hygiene items, duvets and pillows as I felt these would add bulk and help fill the lorry quicker!

But what ended up happening in those two weeks was a true miracle. I was inundated with all the things we had originally asked for plus more. The storage unit filled up with bags which needed sorting and boxes we had packed, and we had to ask for a second storage unit so that we would have the space to sort the clothes as well as somewhere to store them until the lorry came. Our home became a hive of activity and my parents were there every day helping with the children as well as sorting and packing. Each of our downstairs rooms was piled floor to ceiling with bags and boxes.

My patient and long-suffering husband climbed through the towers of brown boxes in the evenings to find a place to sit and watch the TV, after answering the door to volunteers who had turned up to help. Even I didn't know some of the people who were coming to help pack boxes in our house, but I was so grateful to see these kind, smiling strangers at our door.

One day, when there was no more space to move in my

house, I heard my mother gasp. She was staring at a large transit van which had just pulled onto our drive from my son's school.

'Tell them to go away, Samara,' my mother pleaded. 'There is nowhere to put anything else in this house!'

I thanked God for this miracle before opening the front door with a huge smile on my face. I had no idea where we would squeeze this extra van load of bags.

It was an emotional experience sorting through the deluge of clothes. Admiring the best items and gently stroking the beautiful baby clothes we had been given, we imagined the infants who would soon be wearing them. These warm clothes could save the life of someone else's baby. Something about this sorting process appealed to the mother in all of us. At times we found ourselves becoming indignant about dirty or damaged items that had been donated. In sorting and packing these clothes for our brothers and sisters, we felt a connection with them and became rather protective of these people, their dignity and their feelings after the traumatic experiences they had been through.

A memorable moment in this early part of this work was when I was taught a lesson about trust and faith. As a result of the huge flood of clothes received after my prayer of desperation, and having raised an extra £1,000, we sent the lorry to Iraq two and a half weeks early, and I had a room full of boxes left behind. Those leftover boxes were not filled with any of the original items on my list; instead, they were filled with all the extra items I had asked for in my moment of doubt and worry, when I realised how far away I was from my target of ninety cubic metres. God, who has a great sense of humour, had showed me that if I ask him for a miracle, I should expect *him* to deliver it rather than trying to make it happen myself!

After the lorry had been sent, our house group prayed for another miracle: that the aid we had sent would be multiplied, and that there would be enough clothing to serve many thousands of people. In my imagination I had a picture of these boxes being given to people, and of there being more and more boxes of clothes available as the puzzled workers gave them out, rather like the feeding of the five thousand. It is funny looking

back, but in every situation where I have asked God for something, I have always found that what he delivers in response to
our prayers has been far more wonderful than anything I could
have dreamt up in my limited imagination.

God generously answered our prayer for a miracle of even more
items, but he didn't do it my way. The miracle didn't happen out
there in the Middle East as I imagined it would, it happened here
in the UK. Within four years we had sent 109 similar consign-
ments of aid in articulated lorries and forty-foot shipping
containers, which included clothing for hundreds of thousands of
people as well as eleven ambulances. We had sent thousands of
care packs for pregnant and post-natal women, as well as thousands
of dignity bags for women and girls, and hygiene bags with gifts
for children. Additionally, we had provided four small field hospitals at different times and places, to provide life-saving medical
services in Syria. As I considered God's way of achieving an even
more amazing result than I could have envisaged, I realised why
he did it this way and not the way I had imagined.

This work has been about touching lives and I quickly realised it is as important for us here to give as it is for the people
there to receive the aid we send. In the West we live such
comfortable lives and we have a need to share, as much as the
poor have a need for the items we donate. Jesus called us very
specifically to share, and even to sell our possessions to give to
the poor. I believe God wanted to open a door to offer people
in the UK, and in the West, the opportunity to give their
possessions as well as their money. It is better to give than to
receive, and through giving we are blessed.

I believe God wanted to share this blessing of giving in a
practical way with more people. Every one of us has something
to give, whether large or small, or whether it is our time, our
expertise, our resources, our contacts, our clothes or our money.
Each of these things is valuable, and each of these gifts is one
small piece of a much larger picture. The picture is only complete
when every piece is present. When each piece is in its place, the
picture is more beautiful than anything we could create working
alone. It is a beautiful mosaic of team effort and of love.

It was not just about meeting a physical need, it was about serving in love, and in later appeals I was told stories about people who had given very personal items which had great meaning to them. I was extremely moved by the story of one woman who some years previously had given birth to a stillborn baby. She had kept all the clothes she had bought for her child, unable to part with them even years later. However, she was moved to donate them to our appeal, and said that giving in this personal way gave her the opportunity to let go of some of her pain and to let some of her wounds be healed, knowing that in giving these clothes away, someone else's child might be saved as a result.

More than a year later I was touched to see the following message on a good friend's Facebook page after he had helped us load one of our lorries:

We load these up in Sussex. Samara seems to be able to keep filling these lorries and the stuff really does get there (I recognise the banana boxes). There is no company collecting and giving a tiny proportion of the profits, there is no minted chief exec, there are no air-conditioned offices. Your old jumpers go in a banana box here, we put it on a lorry and it goes to some poor person who needs a jumper. The churches seem to be making this colossal network function, for which I am willing to suspend my militant atheism to help because it is going where it is needed, regardless of the recipient's religion. Now go and find an old jumper ...

But after sending the first lorry I felt restless. I saw images of the muddy and miserable camps in Iraq and felt I must do more. I also saw that I couldn't put my family and friends through this same exhausting process again so soon. Everyone had been so supportive, but I knew I had stretched everyone to their limit, as well as myself, in filling an entire lorry of aid for Iraq. I had run out of people of whom I could ask favours. It wouldn't work for me to ask them to do it all again immediately, even if I myself was ready to. I asked God what I should do next.

5

Walking on Water

October 2014 to March 2015

After I asked God for direction, the vision I had was of lots of churches and individuals doing what I had done, but on a smaller, more manageable scale. I would give them instructions as to what to collect, and how to sort, package and label. We would then have a date when everyone would deliver their packed boxes, ready to be loaded onto the lorry. It seemed simple, but I encountered many problems.

After my first big appeal I received a phone bill for £144. My phone usage had multiplied enormously in this time, but it hadn't occurred to me that I could be so far outside my price plan. I couldn't bear to tell my husband, who made all this work possible by supporting our family. I prayed that somehow I could find the money to pay for this as I didn't want to use any of the money raised for this project to cover my expenses. We are in a very good position as a family, but equally, I didn't feel I could ask my husband to pay this bill. I called EE, and for some reason they didn't fully explain, they wrote off most of the money owed and then changed me to a different price plan so that I wouldn't find myself in the same situation again. I was so relieved and thankful.

When I committed in my heart to send a second lorry to Iraq, I quickly began to feel anxious about how I would fill it. After working out the dates, I realised there was just enough time to organise a collection to arrive in Iraq before Christmas. But I began to get cold feet. My previous realisation of the embarrassing shortfall, followed by my prayer of desperation when I felt I had no hope of filling the first lorry, kept playing on my mind. I knew I couldn't fill a second lorry myself in this time frame if God didn't make it happen.

I asked him for a sign. If this time frame was my idea rather than his, I was willing to do the work but wouldn't put myself under the pressure of trying to get the lorry to Iraq before Christmas. If, on the other hand, the pre-Christmas time frame was God's desire, I would work as hard as I could to make it happen in time. I asked him to show me if this was what he wanted by giving me some encouragement that this lorry could be filled and ready by the dates I had planned. I was sure I couldn't do it without him.

Within a couple of hours, I had a call with an organisation that committed to giving around twenty of the ninety cubic metres of clothing needed. This was definite encouragement. The same week, another organisation made a similar commitment. Additionally, some media sources contacted me, rather than me chasing them, wanting to write articles about what I was doing. That week I also had a huge boost with finance being provided for the transport.

Raising £6,500 for the first lorry had been exhausting. The prospect of doing this all over again made me feel tired. I asked God to help because I felt I didn't have the energy or ability to organise any more fundraising events so soon after the last ones. I got talking with an NGO that had just established a UK office and which also collected and sent clothing, as I was doing. It even sent some of its aid to the same partner in Iraq to whom I had sent my first lorry. I said that I planned to send another lorry, and the NGO unexpectedly offered to pay for it, so that I could focus on filling it. This was an enormous blessing and relief!

Each time I looked through the list of churches that were collecting, I became worried that we wouldn't have enough to fill a lorry. I kept remembering the huge volume needed and how it took around twenty volunteers four and a half hours just to load all the boxes onto the vehicle. There was no way of knowing how much or how little we would have at the end of this appeal. I felt as though I was aiming for a target while blindfolded. I had no option but to trust God. It was a strange experience, on the one hand worrying that I couldn't fill this lorry, while, on the other, feeling that the Holy Spirit was telling me to be ready for two lorries. I couldn't make sense of these conflicting feelings.

I had been counting on the same self-storage company for help again as it had been willing to help before, but when I asked it to commit, all of its big units had been rented and it didn't have anything else. I began to panic as it had been a big struggle to find storage the first time, and we were already getting closer to this second deadline. I had no choice but to pray and talk to people about this need. I was put in touch with the managing agents for our local council, who said they might have something suitable. As the agent showed me a perfect unit, exactly the right size for a lorry's worth of boxes, I kept thinking about God's instruction to be ready for two lorries.

'If this filled up and we needed some extra space, you wouldn't by any chance have anywhere else like this, would you?' I felt so cheeky asking.

'Oh yes,' he replied. 'We have another empty one like this upstairs.'

I felt very encouraged by the way this was coming together, and it seemed that these units were available for longer than the couple of weeks we had borrowed the first unit for. I had received so many heartening signs and answers to my prayers. These were so important as we also had many problems to overcome over the next weeks and months.

Well-meaning people packed the boxes with all manner of items which shouldn't have been there, but we only discovered this when I started randomly checking some of the boxes. They could have caused problems with customs if they weren't removed by us and were later discovered at the border. Boxes of chocolates were packed with the clothes, but we would have struggled to be able to gain the right paperwork for customs to include food items being sent into Iraq. In boxes which had been labelled as clothes there were also wedding shoes and accessories, as well as toys and costume jewellery stuffed in the pockets of the clothes. One church that had misunderstood the instructions delivered many bags of items that they had not even looked at, let alone sorted and labelled, and I didn't have the space, volunteers or time to sort and pack them. There were times when I was exhausted and didn't know what to do next.

When the first unit filled up, we spilled into the second unit upstairs. I quickly became concerned that our presence was overwhelming for the occupiers of the surrounding units which were used as offices. To get 1,800 boxes and bags upstairs we either had to carry the boxes one by one up the stairs or stack up the tiny lift before stepping out of it ourselves and then sending it up unaccompanied. We then had to run upstairs to meet it on the first floor and unload it. But even the lift didn't carry much. Well-meaning volunteers kept mistaking the lift's alarm button for the door-opening button, and no one in the building could work out how to turn the alarm off once it started ringing! There were days when the alarm did not stop ringing, and the multitude of vehicles delivering these boxes were clogging up the small parking area, blocking access to the buildings. I soon felt uneasy that the goodwill of our neighbours might, understandably, be starting to wear a little thin.

I was excited when, miraculously, the money was provided for an additional lorry, and we indeed sent off two lorries rather than one. We also had an extra one third of a lorry load of boxes left from the second appeal, which sat in the storage unit over Christmas. That Christmas, my husband asked me, in hope, whether I 'had finished yet'. I hadn't. The truth was, I couldn't stop.

In the first week of January 2015 I launched an appeal for clothing. It snowed in the Middle East the same week, and people in the West were horrified at the sight of displaced people living in camps in the snow. We were inundated with churches and people responding to the appeal. There were now collections across the UK from Cornwall to Scotland, and from Wales to Norfolk. It was spectacular! It had become so big that I felt stretched to my absolute limit.

This was my busiest time yet and I was answering emails until 1.30 a.m. most nights. My children would then wake by 6.30 the next morning, if not before. By God's grace I managed to continue.

In the middle of this busiest time, my computer starting malfunctioning. Certain keys intermittently stopped working, and at this time I sent some very strange emails missing the letters c, e and s! People were very gracious, but it was so frustrating, given how much I needed to try to get done during my brief times at the computer once the children were in bed. I remember praying for my computer to function properly, but I think God had a better plan.

One of the organisations I had been working with called me and said they wanted to give me a donation for my personal expenses. This has never happened before or since. I protested, saying I would much rather put it towards my next lorry, but they insisted. On the day the money arrived in my bank account, the c, e and s keys on my computer completely stopped working for good. I went to PC World the same day to see how much it would cost to buy a new computer as I needed it immediately. It was the exact amount of money the organisation had just paid into my account!

The storage space had been increasingly on my mind again, as we had signed a free lease stating that we would be given two weeks' notice if the units were rented. I talked with many people about this issue, and someone put me in touch with an NGO in Northampton. I was told that this organisation had a warehouse, but as I picked up the phone to call that Friday, I couldn't help wondering how this would help, as I was in Sussex. We were at least two and a half hours' drive from them, and I struggled to find enough volunteers locally, so I didn't see how we would ever manage to find help up there.

The Northampton NGO turned out to be a true blessing. I went to see them after the weekend, and within a week from my first call with them, our boxes and bags were pouring into their warehouse. I was so grateful to their team and volunteers for helping take in those deliveries and helping load up the lorries for me. They didn't realise what they were agreeing to when they said yes to helping me, but they were happily overwhelmed by the volume of boxes which appeared in such a short space of time.

After we had just loaded our first lorry from this warehouse, the NGO's founder told me there were so many boxes being brought that we would need to send another two lorries. It dawned on me as I was processing this news that, for the same reason, I would also need to send another two lorries from Brighton. A prickly sensation crept up my spine. We had just spent another £6,500 on the first lorry we loaded for that January appeal – money which had amazingly been donated by another organisation. Now I only had about £1,000 left, but I was going to need to send at least four more lorries!

After finishing the call, I saw an email from the managing agent of the storage spaces I was using in Brighton. He was apologetic, but said they had a paying customer for both units now and they needed the keys back in two weeks. I had to empty those two units urgently. My mind was racing as I started to process what this entailed. It took around one week to arrange the lorries, which meant I had only one week to find £25,000! It was surreal, and I felt ill thinking about it. I sat down and cried, then told God I wished I had never started doing this work. I prayed another prayer of desperation. What else could I do? I had no other hope at all.

I told God I had no ability to find £25,000, and certainly not in one week. I had struggled to find £6,500 in several weeks! I told him I didn't have anywhere else to move these boxes to, and even if I did, I would need an articulated lorry just to move them, and that would cost money I didn't have. I told God I was tired and I couldn't do it. I said to him I had no one to ask except him, and I wouldn't even know who or where to start asking. I needed his help desperately.

Feeling like a rabbit in the middle of a road staring into the headlights of a car hurtling towards me, I sat in disbelief, brooding over the situation I had managed to get myself into. I thought of the story of the disciples who had fished all night and caught nothing. After Jesus sent them back out to the same place again, they caught so many fish this time that their nets were breaking. After my complete inability to fill my first lorry, I now felt like those disciples, and as though my nets were breaking with the abundance of donations we had received.

I sent one email to the organisation that came to mind first. I was in shock about this overwhelming situation and was unable to do any more than this. I told them of the amazing provision we had received and said that I needed to raise another £25,000. In the email I ran through some calculations, saying maybe I could get a couple of thousand here and maybe a couple there, and perhaps I might be able to raise a little more. I asked whether they might be in a position to contribute some of it. I was praying they might be generous enough to pay for one lorry. When I received an email back within twenty-four hours saying their trustees had agreed to give the full £25,000, I was utterly astounded! I had never hoped or imagined that something like this could be possible, as I certainly hadn't asked them to give all of it.

Those first six months were such a roller coaster of battles, blessings, challenges, opportunities, impossible situations and miracles. It was emotional, and also the most faith-building experience of my life. The heartbreaking situation in the Middle East, the relief of having a way to give, the huge challenges I faced and the amazing encounters with God's grace and provision I experienced were life changing. I learnt what it really meant to step out of the boat and walk on water, and I learnt that every miracle starts with a problem. I also learnt that we should see the challenges we face in life not as problems, but rather as opportunities.

One thing I had never wanted to do at any point in the first few years was set up a charity. I had managed to scrape by working under the umbrella of another charity for the first few months, who were very helpful, but it was far from ideal as there wasn't an obvious way of differentiating our donations from theirs at that time.

It had been during the enormous January appeal that I had a call from Gwyn Williams at Feed The Hungry, kindly offering to collect aid for us too. I was touched that this busy operations director running his own charity was willing to help me with this, and I was intrigued by the work he was doing too. When we finally met, I was so encouraged to find someone else working with a similar prophetic, Spirit-led attitude. I hadn't met many other people who shared the same mentality as me, or who I felt were listening and responding to God faithfully in the same way in this kind of work. It was refreshing also to be able to share and discuss some of the challenges with someone who had a good understanding of all the issues involved in sending aid abroad. Over the coming months we built up a strong partnership which enabled me to work for the next couple of years under the umbrella of their charity.

Gwyn was not only a faith-filled and encouraging charity partner during this time, he was also a great mentor for me, both spiritually and practically. He answered my endless questions, shared numerous documents and protocols, and was a true lifeline and support to me. I don't think anyone else would have been able to work with me in the same way, with the same patience, generosity or trust. I am certain there were times when supporting me and my work pushed him to his limit, and I will always be grateful for the time and support he and the wider US-based organisation, Feed The Hungry, gave me. I can't imagine how the following couple of years would have taken shape without their support. They enabled me to keep focused on the work while they took care of many formalities and oversight. But my work continued to grow and there came a point where I could no longer avoid registering independently as a charity.

Over those months, there were many moments when I worried instead of trusted, and when I looked at my own shortcomings and doubted my ability to complete the work I had started. Over time I have learnt to trust more, but my limited human way of looking at these situations still creeps in. I have learnt that God is good, and that he will provide for all of his work, and that he can give more than I could ever hope to bring to this through my own ability. It is his work, not mine.

Our challenge is that when we pluck up the courage to get out of the boat and start walking on water, it is too easy to be distracted by the wind and the waves, instead of keeping our eyes fixed on Jesus. When we let our eyes drift away from Jesus and instead start to focus on the problems we are facing, we become afraid and we start to sink, as Peter did in Matthew 14:30. We should be absolutely sure that when we are doing God's work, in God's way, there will be many distractions, challenges and difficulties. We should not be put off by these, but accept them as markers that show we are on the right path. When we keep looking to him for the solutions, he rewards us in such an incredible and humbling way.

My experience of answering God's call and doing his work is that he requires us to start walking towards him in an attitude of trust. If we pick up our foot to take a step, seeing nothing in front of us and no place to stand, we should trust that by the time we put our foot back down, there will be something firm underneath for it to land on. When we are selflessly serving God to achieve his plans and not our own, he will give us everything we need. This is the complete opposite of everything we are taught in this world about making plans.

When Jesus sent out his twelve disciples in Matthew 10, Mark 6 and Luke 9, and then later the seventy-two in Luke 10, he gave them very specific instructions. By worldly standards they were foolish, ridiculous, even irresponsible. Who in their right mind would send their team on a mission in which they will clearly be away for some time, at least a few nights if not longer, and tell them not to take any food, nor money, nor a change of clothes, nor even a bag? They were to rely on God, not themselves. He asks us to do the same: 'For the wisdom of this world is folly with God' (1 Cor. 3:19 ESV).

Usually we rely on ourselves, our ability, our resources, our wisdom and our skill to achieve everything. We like to feel in control as this makes us comfortable. But when we surrender everything to God and have nothing left to rely on, and nothing else to give, we have no choice but to depend fully on him, like a child fully depends on their father or mother. This makes us feel vulnerable, weak and uncomfortable, but from God's point of view it makes us ready for him to use, and a perfect vehicle through which he can use his power and strength which is greater and more spectacular than any attribute, skill or resource any of us possess. In 2 Corinthians 12:9 God says to Paul, 'My power is made perfect in your weakness'. Then, in verse 10, Paul acknowledges, 'when I am weak, then I am strong'.

As time went on, I was to experience even more amazing examples of how God's power and provision work best in my weakness. The next spate of incredible events happened when I finally found a Christian NGO in Syria that was able to legally import containers of aid into Syria.

The world wept in September 2015 when photos appeared in the global media of the tiny body of the little Syrian boy Aylan Kurdi washed ashore, face down, on the Turkish coast. This was the point at which people finally began to wake up to the refugee crisis and to what was happening in Syria.

The Syrian conflict had been described by UNHCR, the United Nations Refugee Agency, as producing the 'worst humanitarian crisis of our generation' and as the 'worst manmade disaster since World War II'. It was also described as producing the worst refugee crisis, and at the time little Aylan's body was washed ashore there were also around 6.5 million internally displaced people in Syria who had fled from their homes or whose homes had been destroyed. These internally displaced people may have remained in their home country, but the living conditions of so many of them were no better than those of the people who had fled to neighbouring countries. For many, they were worse, as a lot of people still lived with fighting around them.

My latest appeal had just begun. It was now one year on from my first appeal, and I had spent much time over the summer praying and listening to God about how to progress. My intense anxiety over my previous money issues had been at the forefront of my mind. Even having experienced God's amazing provision in my hours of need, I was scared of finding myself in the same exposed position again. I didn't want another panic over where I could find a huge sum of money while under pressure. I wanted to have the money ready, with everything in place, before I asked people to start collecting. But when I prayed about it, I felt as if God was saying to me, 'I asked you to start collecting first.'

I read two books that summer which encouraged me to step out in faith again: *Birthing the Miraculous* by Heidi Baker, and *Living Water* by Brother Yun. I hadn't planned which two of the many unread books on my shelf to take away and read, yet both of these affirmed similar truths. I read my way through them simultaneously and found that one day I had read a chapter in both books about the same topic – about Mary becoming 'pregnant by the Holy Spirit'. It was fascinating. Submitting to the Holy Spirit is the opposite of doing things the way our culture often teaches us to work.

Remembering God's initial promise to me that if I was willing to step out in faith and start collecting, he would provide everything I needed to make it happen, I felt that submitting to the Holy Spirit was what I should do. Once again, I put myself in his hands. Over the previous year, Syria had remained heavy on my heart and I had been following the relief reports describing the situation there. I had found an NGO in Syria that was experienced in importing containers of aid and that could deal with the legal documents.

I had sent our information pack to all the people who had asked for it, but after the nation's hearts broke for the Syrian toddler who had drowned, we were inundated. I was getting around seventy-five emails each day. So many people wanted to help. I quickly realised that this was already another huge appeal, but I had no way of gauging how many lorries and containers this would translate into.

Once again, I felt as though my nets were at breaking point, and I had three nights lying awake feeling anxious about all the 'what ifs'. My biggest 'what if' was that I might end up with another seven lorries and a container of aid again and have no money to send it all. As each lorry at that time cost around £6,500, this could be a huge amount of money. I had also come down with the worst cold and cough I had ever had, which lasted for more than three months. After my third sleepless night I felt stressed, full of cold and exhausted. I had reached another moment of desperation.

I told God I was so willing to see this appeal through, but I was worried that we would find we had enough aid to send lots of lorries and containers, but no money with which to send them. I asked him once again to give me a little encouragement that the money I needed would be provided. Once again, I thanked him in advance for providing everything that would be needed.

Within a week I had been pledged £35,000 from seven different, reliable donors. It was mind-blowing! After talking with a couple of the donors, however, we decided to spend part of the money on buying the first ambulance I sent to Syria. The rest of the money was nowhere near enough to pay for the twenty-one lorries and containers and the ambulances we would send over the next six months!

Nevertheless, somehow the money just seemed to be there for each container we sent to Syria and for each lorry we sent to Iraq. Money seemed to be coming in to buy ambulances too, and some generous individuals were willing to donate specifically to buy them. By this time, I had also learnt the importance of asking everyone who registered to collect aid for us to also help raise the money needed to transport the boxes they brought to us, and to aim for a specific amount per box. It made a huge difference to my stress levels over the next few years, although on occasion I did still find myself worrying about how we would cover not just the shipping but also the transport and distribution costs in Syria. People were often more keen to collect the clothes than they were to raise the money to send them, but both were needed.

This element of semi-sustainability was essential while the work grew, as I needed to be able to occupy my mind with other challenges and with solving other problems. Sending this aid was a team effort and I felt everyone who helped collect aid should imagine they were sending their own mini container, whether it held twenty boxes or two hundred, and should aim to cover the costs of shipping and distributing their boxes as well as collecting the aid itself.

As a former senior staff nurse in Accident and Emergency, I had increasingly had the medical crisis in Syria on my heart. According to the World Health Organization (WHO), around two thirds of Syria's hospitals either were largely dysfunctional, had closed or had been destroyed. At the same time, the number of war-related deaths was in the hundreds of thousands, and I had seen a report earlier that year stating that there had been more than one million war-related injuries, with tens of thousands of people needing prosthetic limbs. At the time the people of Syria most needed emergency medical care it wasn't available to many. These people needed more than just clothes and hygiene items. They needed life-saving medical care.

After we bought the first ambulance, an NGO in Syria connected me with a Syrian Christian doctor working on the ground. It was important for me to understand the situation in the field if I wanted to encourage others to help. I could never have anticipated how, over time, this doctor living on another continent in such a different culture, whose world was so unlike mine, would become not just an immensely strong colleague in this work, but also one of my closest friends. His family became my family. Two of his beautiful children were the same ages as mine. Each time I visited Syria, I was welcomed by him and his wife, eating with them, sleeping in their home, playing games with their children. They treated me as one of their family.

6

Dr A

'It is a true war here, Samara. This is a real battle.' I could feel the unease in his voice. 'Maybe I should give you my wife's number, in case something happens to me.'

I was silent as I digested the significance of Dr A's words. He carried a huge weight of responsibility. My heart was undone. He was talking about life and death. He was talking about his family. He was talking about real fear, not the day-to-day worries which we occupy ourselves with here in the UK. Since the crisis began, he had seen and dealt with death, with appalling injuries, and with situations and sights most people would never see in a lifetime. He had seen the very worst of what humanity is capable of, often on a daily basis.

As well as dealing with this disaster as a doctor, as an individual he was also living in the middle of all the killings and kidnappings, seeing the rape victims and experiencing the savage bombs that were exploding around him, his home and his family. He faced the terrifying sounds of guns, explosions and fighting and the chronic stress and uncertainty which accompanied it all.

We had spoken many times before, but our conversations had mostly been focused on the details of our work, the situations in the hospitals, the patients the hospitals were dealing with, and how we might help. We exchanged lots of messages about medical equipment, about what was useful and what might pose a problem with customs. But this was the first time I had stopped to consider fully the depth of what all this meant for him as a human being, as a husband, father and son, not just as a doctor or professional serving in this war-ravaged land.

Dr A came from a poor family in Syria and his early years

were characterised by enormous challenges. The family just about managed to make ends meet, but it was a struggle. He and his siblings were the only Christians at his school, and Dr A gained top marks in each subject, a combination which resulted in many difficulties for them, including persecution. Even in studying the Qur'an at school, he gained better marks than his Muslim classmates, who came to him when they had questions about their own religion.

Dr A excelled in his studies and was awarded a scholarship to study without charge at a medical school in Syria that took the students with the highest grades. Much of his English was self-taught, but he chose to study his medical textbooks in English rather than Arabic, systematically reading his way through them during his hour-long bus ride each way to medical school every day. After leaving medical school he worked in some of the best hospitals in Syria, gaining essential experience in the areas he was to specialise in, and became a successful doctor.

One of the most remarkable things about Dr A is that he did the opposite to what most other Syrian people did at the start of the conflict. When the fighting began in earnest, he had been working on a short medical contract outside Syria, but as it became clear that big troubles were beginning and that war was breaking out, he felt called to return to his country. The company he was working for tried to persuade him not to go back, but rather to bring his family out of Syria to a safer place. They offered him high-value contracts to encourage him not to return. At the time, most people who could were leaving Syria. But as a doctor who had trained for free in Syria, he felt that his calling was to return and do the work he had trained for all his life. His people needed him, and he was sure Syria was exactly where God wanted him to be.

With my background as a nurse in emergency care, we instantly connected. As he brought me up to speed on the issues they faced, I felt ashamed remembering how I had complained in my nursing days about the working conditions in the hospitals in the UK. I could not understand how they worked at all in Syria with so few resources when they had to deal with so many serious injuries. I felt for the staff as much as for the patients who had sustained such horrific injuries.

One day, I sent Dr A some footage I had seen showing what seemed like an infinite amount of destruction in one of the Syrian cities. It was overwhelming, and I asked him if he and his family really lived in this country. He replied in his characteristically strong and optimistic way.

'Do you know the story of the phoenix? We are Phoenician here in Syria. We will rise from the ashes and rebuild.' I was always inspired by his ability to be so positive in the middle of what seemed to be a living hell on earth.

The day he told me it was a true war there, however, Dr A's voice had lost the positive confidence with which I had become familiar. A massive bomb had exploded in a crowded place. The attack was carried out in the city by terrorists who had filled a car with nearly one tonne of explosives. Fifteen were killed immediately and more than fifty sustained multiple injuries. Many buildings were also destroyed, along with several ambulances. His voice sounded so weary.

'It is a nightmare, Samara. Many children are buried with their Christmas gifts under fallen buildings. It is so bad. We can't explain what happened to the fathers or mothers or children. It is a nightmare.'

Two weeks later one of their emergency medical teams, made up entirely of civilian medics, attended the scene of another car bomb attack which killed nine and wounded four. But a suicide bomber was waiting for them at the scene. As the medical team started to treat the wounded, a jihadist stood in their midst and detonated his explosive vest. Among others, three of the medics were seriously injured. The emergency doctor sustained multiple injuries including a severe, permanent brain injury. She never walked or worked again.

A week later, Dr A told me they were dealing with multiple cases of influenza which had resulted in numerous people dying of multi-organ failure. They had no ability to isolate people in their hospitals or to carry out proper diagnostics in a timely manner, and the staff were becoming sick as a result. One of their staff caught influenza and subsequently died. In his hospital they were doubling up patients on the same pieces of equipment as they didn't have enough. None of these things were new for Dr A, as parts of his city had seen some of the worst bombing, fighting, sieges and destruction since early in the conflict. But the medical crisis had consistently worsened throughout the war, and they, like most other hospitals in Syria, had not been able to replace worn-out equipment or buy anything new. Expectations sank lower and lower as they became accustomed to continually deteriorating circumstances as time went on.

Early in the conflict two hospitals had been taken by jihadist groups. They killed and beheaded the Christian and Shia doctors who had been working there. Some of those doctors were Dr A's friends and colleagues – ordinary civilians, doctors whose focus was on saving the lives of others. These hospitals were taken over by these armed groups who allegedly used them as military bases from where they fired rockets into the surrounding areas, killing men, women and children.

Dr A had a good friend, Dr Issa, who had been a partner in a private hospital. He had invested an enormous amount of time and money in that hospital, choosing and buying the best equipment, and training the staff to work to a high standard. The people from the area felt sure the other doctors who became radicalised had been planning what ended up happening there for a long time.

Dr Issa, along with the other Christian and Shia doctors, was forced out of this hospital by extremist Muslim doctors with whom he had worked for a long time. They had gained his trust over time. They, along with others, had been listening to the teachings of influential Islamist sheikhs. Many people in the area, as well as across Syria, had become radicalised by the teachings of these sheikhs, who were broadcasting from TV channels across Syria. In the locations which these and other extremist armies had started to control, people who were not in support of their ideology were forced out of their workplaces and homes.

Before the conflict began, some of the doctors that Dr Issa

had been working with had started asking him how much he
would pay as a ransom if he was kidnapped. He hadn't known
what to think about these inexplicable comments coming from
people he knew. They began trying to pressure him to sell them
his home, a nice house in an expensive area, for a token amount
of money such as $100, telling him he should sell it because he
would soon lose it anyway. These comments were so strange
and bizarre, it was hard for him to know how to respond or
what they meant.

One day, he had a phone call warning him not to go to his
hospital under any circumstances, even if they called him and
told him there was an emergency. The situation had been rapidly
deteriorating, so he heeded this advice, not wanting to take any
chances. That day, these radicalised doctors and the jihadist group
they were connected with took over the hospital, taking staff
and patients hostage. This group allegedly went on to use the
hospital as a military base, attacking the surrounding areas from
it. The entire hospital was soon destroyed.

Soon after this, Dr Issa and his wife began to feel very uncomfortable in their own home as they lived in an area where the
tensions and hostilities had increased, and it was clear that an
extremist faction was emerging. They began to feel intimidated
by these people, and by the activities taking place around them.
One Friday they tried to go for a walk in their local park with
their children, but they saw a large group of men with long
beards and women in hijabs blocking their way. As Dr Issa's wife
was not covered, this group started shouting abusive comments
at them for being Christian. They felt afraid as they didn't know
what might happen next. They decided to stay in a different
area until the situation calmed. But it didn't calm. Instead, Dr
Issa soon received a call telling him not to return to his home
as it had been taken by the Islamists controlling the area and
had been given to one of their families. The whole area was
taken over by these armed extremists, and Dr Issa and his family
were some of the lucky ones who managed to get out alive.

He protested to the Islamists when they called him, and told
them that all their clothes and belongings were in the house.

But he was told that if he went back, they couldn't guarantee he wouldn't be killed. This was the first of many times Dr Issa and his family, along with many others in the same situation, moved home during the conflict. The people in Syria couldn't understand what was happening around them, but then many of the extremists began to carry heavy weapons in the street, and were joined by foreign militants, attacking and killing policemen and civilians, and taking people's homes and neighbourhoods. Similar atrocities were seen taking place in other cities and villages across the country, and the conflict quickly descended into a full-scale war.

Some of the hospitals where Dr A worked were brought the bodies of many of the victims. These were civilian hospitals, and the dead were people who had been killed by the jihadist armies that took nearby areas by force, as well as by the brutal bombings and fighting which ensued to try to force those fighters back out. They received many victims of torture and beheadings, and they were left with the inconceivable task of suturing the heads back onto these bodies so that their families could take them away to bury. It was a tremendously sensitive issue, yet there were times when they were brought so many corpses it was very difficult to find the right head for each body. There were times when they simply couldn't.

The situation deteriorated to such an unthinkable low that sometimes the relatives of those who had died would, in spite of their grief, express their gratitude for having a body in one piece to bury. They considered themselves to be luckier than some of their neighbours whose relatives had been mutilated. Many never saw or heard from their loved ones again.

Kidnappings became commonplace. Even in safer areas many people stopped travelling after dark or avoided certain areas or roads where many people had been taken. A number of Dr A's friends and colleagues had been kidnapped. Many of them were killed, and in a lot of cases these individuals were used to extract ransoms. The most successful doctors – and anyone else known to be wealthy, or at least comfortably off – were targeted. Sometimes kidnappings, which resulted in beatings, torture and sometimes repeated rape, even of men, were also used as a way to humiliate and break people down if they spoke out against the jihadist groups that were responsible for so much ruthless inhumanity. On one occasion when Dr A was travelling to visit his parents in a different area, he was warned on the way that one of the groups in this area planned to kidnap him. Apparently, he was told, they had promised to treat him well. It was years before he made that journey again.

A couple of weeks after these recent bombings and the influenza outbreak, I received a message from Dr A saying that there had been another terrorist bombing just 500 metres from his house. Forty-five were killed and more than one hundred injured. Victims were carried to the hospitals in people's arms and in the back of pick-up trucks as they didn't have enough ambulances. The maimed and blood-soaked victims were crowded into the hospital corridors and the staff were overcome by the horror of what they were seeing.

The trauma for the staff was exacerbated by their physical inability to cope with a major incident like this. There was no medical support or back-up, and they didn't have the resources to provide meaningful help for such a huge influx of severely injured people all needing urgent care at the same time for significant and life-threatening injuries. Many of the nurses, he told me, wished they could have swapped places with the patients: watching this meaningless misery with no ability to help or explain it was unbearable, and seemed, in some bizarre way, to be worse than being on the receiving end of these horrific injuries.

At the time, two of their paramedics had just died of swine flu. In another explosion, a friend's house had been damaged. When Dr A called to check if he was OK, his friend said his home, where he was sitting talking to him on the phone, had been hit by the bomb. One of the walls had been blown off. He told Dr A he would eat his lunch and then call him back.

'Can you imagine?' he asked me in disbelief. 'He is sitting in his house which has just been bombed, and he wants to eat his lunch before he talks with me? He is a dead man waiting for his turn.'

This was a phrase I would become familiar with over the next few months. Over time and with repeated exposure to death, near misses and continuous fighting, many Syrian people living in the most war-ravaged areas stopped trying to run from death. Instead they stared it in the face, defiantly living with resignation, accepting the consequences, whatever they may be. Some even saw death as a welcome escape from the hell they had been living in over the last few years. Some of the survivors felt as if, for the dead, their problems were finally over. They had had their way out. It was just the people left behind who were in anguish and who had to pick up the pieces and keep suffering, living in this hell on earth.

But this big bomb attack so close to Dr A's home, with its many complications, preceding events and surrounding circumstances, was a crescendo of agony, and became a defining moment in our friendship. After this attack something changed. Dr A had always seemed like a pillar of strength, but after a day so horrific it was beyond anyone's ability to ever imagine, he was openly fatigued and vulnerable. After communicating many of the traumas of this nightmare day, with no medical support available, his message at the end simply said: 'Samara, I am alone.'

Over the years, and given the relentless nature of the continuing conflict, he had become worn down and exhausted. His energy was depleted, and he was running on empty. With no sign of light at the end of the tunnel, the lack of hope had begun to eat away at the souls of the people who were surrounded by the worst of the worst situations. His fatigued anger at the injustice of so much suffering, and at his powerlessness to make a real difference, was burning. One big difference between the English and Middle Eastern mentalities is that men from the latter culture are more inclined to express their feelings. When he was upset, angry or frustrated, he was open about it. This made it easier for me to try to understand and offer some level of support.

He tried to protect me, however, from the awfulness of the hell they were living in. He worried that if he said too much or told me all the real details, I would not be able to cope with what I was hearing, and he would push me too far, perhaps scaring me off.

At the end of a tough day in a small hospital where he had been working, in an area that had been under attack, he described the children with body parts missing, the man choking to death on his own blood, and the two people with serious brain injuries who they were unable to transfer to another hospital in the city for the urgent specialist care they needed. One of them died and the other was left in a 'bad situation'. Relatives of patients at this small hospital were fighting over who got to be transferred in the ambulance to the larger hospital in the city. On some days they would squeeze twelve patients into one ambulance, some sitting, some standing, with corpses being laid on the floor to be taken to the mortuary, for the couple of hours' drive to the nearest city hospital across the rough and dangerous road.

Two of their ambulances had broken down because of the challenging road conditions in this area. There were also fuel shortages as so many fuel-producing areas were under the control of jihadist groups, and international sanctions restricted fuel supply from other parts of the world, meaning that they were unable to get their logistics running efficiently. The poor quality of the only available fuel caused damage to the engines, and at this time the ambulances kept breaking down. These ambulances were like worn-out, starved, old workhorses being flogged to death in the hope that a little more service could be squeezed out of them.

If these events weren't enough, one of Dr A's friends was then killed by a sniper bullet, leaving behind a wife and three children. At the end of this day, he told me in an exhausted voice, 'I'm tired of death. So many people from my life have left the country or died. I feel as though everyone has gone. I am alone here.'

Over the time we had been in contact I had spent a lot of time trying to encourage him. In the early days I felt woefully inadequate as I tried to find some kind of supportive words or encouragement to offer. I had never experienced any level of conflict or death. What could I, with my naïve experience of such a comfortable life in a safe country, possibly say to encourage someone who had witnessed so many of the most evil atrocities imaginable? What did I know about living through this kind of suffering and trauma? Yet, somehow, he appreciated these humble efforts.

It was a release for Dr A to be able to talk with someone outside the situation they were all drowning in, who was not weighed down and burnt out by living through the same traumas that he was experiencing. As well as running his own organisation, hospitals and medical points and being a senior partner in another larger hospital, he had the additional pressure of needing to keep a strong and encouraging face for his team, as well as for his family. I started a prayer group, and we quickly had a very faithful collection of people who would pray about the biggest challenges and problems, with many who would also fast. Over the years, Dr A has grown as fond of this faithful prayer group as the group has of him.

Through this period, I shared with Dr A passages and encouraging stories from the Bible of people and prophets who had also suffered yet achieved amazing things, as well as inspiring stories of more recent Christians I had read about who had also lived through very traumatic or challenging experiences. At this time, we began to talk in much greater depth about our faith. He came from a very faithful and spiritual Catholic family, and from our conversations it was clear he had a detailed knowledge of parts of the Bible, and a very strong, trusting and inspiring faith in God. But I could see he missed a personal relationship with Jesus, and had yet to experience being filled with the Holy Spirit.

Some evenings after he got home from the hospital, we would start discussing our work and then talk for hours about the teachings of Jesus and what we felt they should look like in our lives, about events which took place in the Old Testament, as well as about other aspects of the Bible, Christianity and the differences between our faith and Islam. He was hungry to know exactly what I believed and why, and seemed satisfied that my actions in life seemed to match my words and my expressed beliefs. His previous experiences of religious people had been very disillusioning, and he was very sceptical of anyone in a position of religious leadership. He had grown tired of religious leaders who talked the talk but didn't walk the walk, or perhaps who didn't even talk the talk. He was weary of hypocrisy and of religious leaders who would try to evangelise, but whose actions served themselves rather than the poor. He was tired of seeing corruption in the Church, and of not seeing the evidence of these people's faith in the way they lived their lives.

Perhaps to our benefit, I was not in such a position. I was just a simple Christian, a mother of two, trying to follow God's calling to serve. We analysed many passages in the Bible in great detail. I felt that each of these conversations shifted something in his heart, which jumped in recognition, like a reminder of something he had forgotten a long time ago. One day when we were talking about our faith, he simply said, 'You have something I need. I don't know what it is.'

'It's Jesus,' I replied.

One evening we prayed over the phone, and when it got late, we said goodnight. In the morning I found a message from him saying he had continued praying for a couple of hours after we said goodbye. He described it as being truly beautiful, like being in heaven. He hadn't even been sure which language he was praying in.

Over the next few months, I saw his heart beginning to be healed from the hurt and anger which had been so consuming in those early days. It was incredible to see the difference between who and where he was when we were first introduced and the very different man I knew so well a few years later. He came to know Jesus, not just as God, but in a personal way, and the Holy Spirit was so clearly in his heart, guiding his decisions and actions. God works many different kinds of miracles, but those which heal the heart are the most beautiful and moving to witness. There are few Christians I know whose faith I respect and admire as much as Dr A's. It is like gold refined by the most intense fire.

Around the time we started talking about opening our first small field hospital together, there had been much discussion, but we had not yet made a commitment to it. One day, he told me he wanted to know what God was saying to me about it when I prayed, and said he knew what God had said to him. When I asked him what God had told him, he went on to describe in great detail a prophecy God had given him shortly before we were introduced. There were many fascinating elements to it, but the last part said: 'I will send you a star from the desert to guide you and help you in your journey.'

He then told me that Samara is a name common among the Bedouin people who live in the desert, and then asked, 'Is it you, Samara?'

How I should begin to answer a question like that, I did not know.

7

Our First Field Hospital

2016–17

'All the hospitals have been destroyed. There is nothing left.' Dr A's voice sounded exhausted. One of those destroyed was a hospital he had worked with. Although we hadn't spoken before about the obvious, he must have known in his heart even before he saw the ruins that it would not have been left intact. Yet knowing in your heart and seeing with your eyes are very different things. When you have not seen, you can cling to a little hope, whether rational or not, that something will be OK. Maybe the building will be OK. Maybe ISIS would have fled too quickly to have done any damage. Maybe some of the equipment would still be there. His despair at having his hopes dashed was amplified further by the knowledge that this small hospital, had it remained intact, could have been a lifeline for many poor and traumatised people who would otherwise be left to die.

When ISIS had first attacked this area it came like a thunderbolt. It was an enormous shock, and the fighting was intense. Many men, women and children were killed. Homes, buildings and cars were destroyed. That hospital dealt with a huge number of the injured. The team there, as well as people from the area, called people outside asking for support and resources, but these were difficult times. There had been snipers outside stopping helpers from reaching the hospital with the supplies needed.

No one believed that ISIS would take this area, and sure enough, their attacks were subdued after much fighting. People were celebrating the victory that ISIS had been defeated. The situation began to improve and the original hospital, along with other resources in the area, was replenished as soon as it was safe to access. People were desperate for help after the terrible losses and life-changing ordeals they had just been through. Those from surrounding areas were keen to help them recover. Lots of medication and supplies were sent to help. Just as everyone was breathing a sigh of relief, without warning, the area fell completely to ISIS.

Many people secretly working with ISIS had been based in the area for a long time. They lay low, biding their time until the opportunity came for them to pursue their true agenda. These people won the trust of the local people, gaining positions in key places well ahead of time, then used these positions to assist ISIS and enable it to take full control of the area.

At the beginning ISIS didn't appear to interfere with the hospital. The team had closed the doors, and most of the doctors and team fled. Others disappeared. Around this time, much of the surrounding communication infrastructure was destroyed, making it hard to maintain contact with anyone in the surrounding areas. The situation was chaotic and confused, and it was hard for anyone to know what was really happening. Many of the hospital's medical team became uncontactable and it was hard to know who was dead, who was alive, who was out of range, and who was hiding.

One of the people whom Dr A could not contact was one of the doctors working in the hospital. He had been reliable and committed, polite, respectful and hard-working. When the area had been under attack from ISIS, he had vowed to die there rather than leave.

Dr A lost contact with him when ISIS took control, and he was worried about what had happened to him. He knew what jihadist armies did to doctors in the hospitals they took. He had lost many friends this way, and was extremely troubled.

Soon, word came back from the local people. The doctor was alive. The local people said he had re-opened the hospital under his own authority, this time serving ISIS. They felt he had been committed to their agenda all along, first gaining this strategic position in the area, as well as the trust of the team and the local people, then restocking the hospital during the pause for breath, and then waiting for the opportunity to take over.

He betrayed the people he had worked with in the hospital who were not Sunni Muslims – 'infidels', as they called them. ISIS fighters went to the homes of two of the nurses and beheaded them. Other people disappeared, and no one found out what happened to them. Many questions still remain unanswered, and numerous people are still unaccounted for. No one could get into the area to verify the situation or find out what happened.

At this time, Dr A's heart filled with dread at the sound of his phone ringing. He had lost so many friends and colleagues over a relatively short space of time, and so many terrible things happened during this period, that he had every reason to fear the worst each time the phone rang.

When he travelled to the newly freed area, he found the hospital he had worked with destroyed and the equipment gone. After the fight to free the city, no one really knew who had destroyed what. Dr A was shocked to hear that some equipment had been taken by the people who were supposed to be protecting it. The whole situation had deteriorated into a disordered mess. The lack of law and order, the influence of the jihadist groups, the collapsed economy, and people's need to eat meant that the boundaries between good and bad, right and wrong had become blurred or, for many, completely worn away.

The personal betrayals have been some of the most painful, incomprehensible trials for the Syrian people to come to terms with. Even at the time of writing this, the people I meet in Syria say they can't understand or believe what happened in their country. Their neighbours, the people they went to school with, worked with and had known all their lives, became radicalised and were suddenly part of movements like ISIS, Jabhat al-Nusra, and the Free Syrian Army to name a few. They used to eat meals and drink tea with each other, then one day those same people were kidnapping and ransoming or killing them. Any Christians, Shia or Druze – anyone rejecting their ideology. Their wives and daughters were raped, their homes were taken, and many of them were beheaded. Trust between people in Syria reached an all-time, rock-bottom low.

Some families had remained in this area during the reign of

ISIS, but most had fled. It was estimated that there were thousands of people living there after ISIS was forced out. Once the area was liberated, many more returned.

Having sent much medical equipment and several ambulances to Syria, I had started talking with Dr A about a new subject: opening a small field hospital. By British standards, a hospital like this would be extremely primitive, but after years of conflict and sanctions, and with the loss of effectively around two thirds of the hospitals in Syria (according to the WHO), it would be life-saving.

We had discussed a couple of locations. The fact that this particular area had been liberated before we had committed to a location seemed important. There was no remaining hospital there, and the nearest one was a long way away. Areas further afield were still under ISIS and jihadist control and were inaccessible. The families living in this liberated area were poor, and many would struggle to make the journey to the nearest city. Displaced people were expected to start returning now the area was free.

We therefore decided to open our first field hospital in this newly freed area. Initially, after the siege, there was no running water or electricity, so we had to take in tanks of water as well as run a generator to provide the services needed. An added complexity was that it wouldn't be possible to find a medical team to resource the hospital among the local residents. Doctors and nurses had to be driven in from outside the area, to work, sleep and live there for a week, and then be replaced a week later by another team.

Dr A recruited a team of doctors and nurses willing to help in this area, even though it was still dangerous. Even among the Syrians who remained in the country through the conflict, it took a certain kind of person to work in a place like this. Dr A worked day and night for weeks to get the building prepared, negotiating for all the equipment, and arranging the transport and the team. He did an amazing job establishing it.

Although our team felt safe from ISIS because there was military protection, it takes time to re-establish law and order after the social and legal infrastructure of an area has been completely destroyed. In the weeks and months before we established this hospital, a medical team at another small hospital Dr A worked with, experienced problems when groups of armed fighters would arrive demanding treatment. His staff had been attacked by these armed groups. We were concerned about this happening at the new hospital too, and had a security team in place for this reason, but thankfully we did not have any problems during our time there.

Around the time I first started sending aid to Syria, I had contact with a few NGOs recommended by other Christian charities outside Syria, and formed a partnership with one of them. Over time I did not feel they were working with the same heart as I was. After praying and fasting about this partnership, I was given some prophetic words from people who didn't know the situation, about 'moving camps'.

Some time before being given these messages, I was introduced to Dr A, and began to build up a high level of trust working with him. We communicated regularly for many months, and for much of this time we were in contact daily, usually engaged in detailed and lengthy discussions about different aspects of our work. I got to know him well and could see that he was true to his word even when there were problems. I had seen his heart, and had already walked through some tough times with him, but I felt the weight of responsibility to not simply trust my own judgement or instincts, but also to diligently cover and be sure of everything we were doing. Directing money that has been generously donated by people, and given in good faith and love, is a huge duty not to be taken lightly.

Dr A had always gone much further than I had asked of him in terms of reporting and acting with due diligence, as well as in the care and meticulousness with which he implemented every project. He didn't cut corners and was reliable in every commitment he made. When the hospital was being prepared, I received daily photos and videos from him showing how the work was proceeding: the empty building at the start, the doorways widened, the emergency entrance, walls knocked down inside to make it useable, as well as information about how and where each department was organised, including the furniture and equipment. The evidence spoke volumes.

When working at a distance, a huge amount of trust is required, and it takes time to build this. At that point I had not yet visited Syria. I was about to start asking our supporters whether they would be willing to give regular assistance to this hospital, and I needed to be confident that I had done everything correctly and left no stone unturned. On paper I had indeed done this. In fact, we had gone much further in terms of reporting and acting with due diligence than I have seen other NGOs doing. At the time I asked God to give me very clear assurance that I was following the right path, so that I could be completely sure that it was his wisdom to invest more in this partnership. I was willing to follow God's guidance, no matter what it was, as long as I could be absolutely sure I was following his path.

One Saturday morning in May, a week before the hospital opened, I asked God to show me what the situation was. I asked him to give me a sign: something crystal clear so that I could have complete confidence. I needed to be able to give my full attention to the big task ahead.

After praying, I felt impatient for an answer, as I hadn't felt the earth move or God's voice giving any direction. I removed the page marker from my Bible, fanning the pages with my eyes closed. I asked God to show me something which made sense to me in this situation, to guide me and direct me. Randomly, I stopped fanning and opened the pages. When I opened my eyes, the first place they fell was on 2 Chronicles 9. I could hardly believe what I was reading. In front of me was the passage where the Queen of Sheba visits King Solomon. The whole passage was interesting, but the specific verses that stood out to me were 1–6:

> When the queen of Sheba heard of Solomon's fame, she came
> to Jerusalem to test him with hard questions. When she met
> with Solomon, she talked with him about everything she had
> on her mind. Solomon had answers for all her questions; nothing
> was too hard for him to explain to her. When the queen of
> Sheba realised how wise Solomon was, and when she saw the

palace he had built, she was overwhelmed. She exclaimed to the king, 'Everything I heard in my country about your achievements and wisdom is true! I didn't believe what was said until I arrived here and saw it with my own eyes. In fact, I had not heard the half of your great wisdom! It is far beyond what I was told.'

The symbolism in this passage was immediately easy to identify with. The scenario describes a foreign woman visiting Solomon in order to 'test him with hard questions'.

I was amazed reading this passage, as it described a similar situation to mine. The Queen of Sheba wanted reassurance that she truly understood the situation, so she went to see for herself. All her concerns were addressed when she met and talked with Solomon, and she was clearly impressed by everything she saw.

I then reread the passage many times, as it completely addressed the issue of reassurance as well as that of partnership. The Queen of Sheba gave King Solomon many valuable gifts, some of which he used to build steps to the temple. I felt this passage had answered my anxieties about needing to be sure of the situation. I would probably have felt reassured by something less specific, but this was really moving, and I felt emotional reading it.

Still feeling emotional, I flipped to a different part of the Bible, where I came across a passage which talked about an area that was rebuilt. As I read it, I felt bewildered, as it was the name of the very area where we were planning on opening our small hospital the following week! I hadn't even known that this place was mentioned in the Bible, and when I spent time researching it, I found that this is the only place in the Bible translation I was using where this area is mentioned. I could barely believe it!

I was overwhelmed as I tried to process how generous God is with us. I would have been happy just to have been directed to the passage describing the visit of the Queen of Sheba, or just to have been shown the verse about this area being rebuilt, where we were opening our first field hospital. To see both of them, after asking God to show me something to reassure me and confirm that I was following the correct path, felt mind-blowing.

Astonished by this experience, I called Dr A to tell him. By this time, we had developed such an honest partnership and friendship that I knew I could tell him what had happened without it causing us problems. He too was amazed by these passages that were so specific – though we also couldn't help laughing about the symbolism of the characters described in them!

There have been other instances when I have used this way of trying to gain an answer from God about a specific situation – that is, by praying, and then opening the Bible randomly. I should point out that no church, Christian leader or anyone else has suggested this to me as a means of listening to God. It is not something I am recommending as a model to use as a way of hearing from him, it is just something I began doing, usually in situations when I felt in need of an answer about something very important relating to my work serving him. Often at these times I have felt impatient to know what I should do, and God, in his generosity, has answered me in many of those moments, especially the most pressing, but he has not answered in every situation – and I don't use this way for making all important decisions, just some. I have always prayerfully weighed these passages that I find in front of me.

The situation we have been dealing with in Syria has been rather unique, and certainly dangerous at times, and perhaps this is the reason God has engaged with us in this unusual way. My recommendation is that people study the Bible to understand the fundamental meanings and contexts of each book and chapter, which I do too. This is what enables us to develop in understanding and wisdom, and in our relationship with God.

Yet I have also found that through asking God for guidance and listening to him in this way, my knowledge and understanding of the Bible, and of God's character, have grown deeper. In the past, I was more interested in reading the New Testament. I found the Old Testament harder to relate to and I didn't know or understand as much about events recounted in parts of it. But during these years, I have really felt God speaking to me, to *us*, through the Old Testament, and in a way that has brought it vividly to life. It is not simply a historical document, it is God's living Word. His Word is alive today. It is interactive, and it is truly a lamp for our feet (as expressed in Psalm 119:105). I don't know why he has chosen to use this way of speaking with me, but my feeling is that he wanted me to engage with his Word in greater depth. The Bible is the most exciting, amazing book I have ever read. Many people think of it as dull or full of violence and anger, but this misses its message and meaning, as it is really the most beautiful love story ever written.

Even though there may not be a biblical precedent for asking God for guidance and then opening the Bible randomly, hoping for an answer, I believe that the master and creator of the universe can choose how he communicates with each of us, and that our position is to listen carefully, pray for discernment, and be open to what he wants to say to us, however he chooses to do it. Whether he speaks to us through the Bible, in an audible voice, through dreams, through visions, through prophecies from another Christian, through pictures, or straight to our hearts, we should always be ready to listen, and to hear him.

Four months later, I had a further validation. Working from a distance as we had been doing requires a high level of trust, and we certainly had that. But I felt that perhaps God wanted to endorse the importance and nature of our partnership once again, as well as to give some guidance about being prepared to weather some of the storms which lay ahead.

One evening when I was talking with Dr A on the phone, we were discussing our partnership, and he was making some comments and statements which I was brushing off rather dismissively. He described our partnership as being like a gear, with the metal teeth of both wheels needing to fit together in a precise way, in exactly the right position, for the mechanism to turn correctly and work, and he observed that one wheel can't work with a different wheel that it wasn't designed to work with.

While we were talking, my laptop chirped as an email came through. I saw that it was from a woman who had been very committed to collecting aid for us, as well as organising events promoting awareness about our work and the situation in Syria.

She had been one of our regular prayer team and was often willing to fast and pray with us over some of the bigger things. The subject of the email said 'fasting', but as I was in the middle of this conversation, I didn't open it. At the end of our conversation, I was tired and went straight to bed. My emails could wait until the morning.

When I woke the next morning, I checked my emails on my phone. I stared in disbelief at the picture in the email I had received the night before while Dr A had been describing the teeth of the metal wheel fitting together. In the email was an image of exactly what he had described to me. These two people had never had any contact with each other, and one was in Syria and the other in the UK. The text of the email read:

Dear Samara

Apologies for not forwarding earlier, but just wanted reassurance before doing, but believe I should trust and hand over in faith.

At the end of a day of fasting a few Sundays ago (21st Aug) I believe God gave me a picture for you of some bevel gears.

All the work and effort and fundraising you are driving is represented by the driving gear on the left, turning in a set direction, but when this gear hits the 2nd, it triggers a change of direction.

The purpose of bevel gears is to change direction of a shaft's rotation.

Here are a few facts about these types of gears:

- One wheel of such gear is designed to work with its complementary wheel and no other.
- Must be precisely mounted.
- The shafts' bearings must be capable of supporting significant forces.

My prayer is that God will guide and direct you in all wisdom – trust He will speak to you through this picture.

I was stunned to receive this email, and especially to see what the woman had written about this gear. What overwhelmed me even more was the time she had sent it. She had been fasting and praying and had received this picture two and a half weeks before sending the email. Then, she had made the extraordinary decision to send it at the same time Dr A was inspired to describe our partnership using the exact same imagery and detail. It felt surreal.

I immediately forwarded the email on to Dr A and apologised if I had seemed a little flippant the evening before concerning his comments about our partnership. We were astounded by both the image description and the timing of this email. Later, I called the woman who sent the picture and asked her more about it before telling her of its significance. She said that, coming as she did from an engineering background, she knew there were a number of unique points about this kind of gear, but the features she had listed had been the ones she felt were especially relevant to the picture she had while fasting.

We have found many times through this work that God responds to us in a very interesting and personal way when we humble ourselves enough to fast and focus on prayer and on spending time with him. I don't really know how or why this is, but there is something about the change of concentration and attitude which takes place when we fast that enables us to draw closer to God. We focus more on him, and connect with him in prayer in a way that doesn't always come as naturally when we are not fasting. Perhaps this should not come as a surprise, as throughout the Bible we see examples of key biblical figures and prophets such as Moses, Daniel, Esther and even

Jesus fasting before big events took place and of key prophetic visions which have been received while fasting to warn people of coming events.

Fasting is also something I have found very difficult to do at times, and the temptation is always to end sooner than I originally planned. Yet after fasting for a couple of days, I feel so much more open to hearing from God, and find it so much easier to devote myself to praying and listening to him. It often helps to have others fasting at the same time about the same issue as there is a feeling of togetherness, and I also feel it is important to try to do it when you can take time to concentrate on praying, reading the Bible and listening to God. Days when the children are at school are much more effective than those when they are at home. I do still drink water when I fast, but I won't have anything else.

I feel that fasting is something all of us should try to do occasionally in our journey in faith, although you might need to approach it more carefully if you have a medical condition that would make it more difficult.

8

I Was Sick, and You Cared for Me

May to December 2016

The medical crisis in Syria has been globally unique in its size, scale and escalation. In 2016, WHO stated that almost two thirds of the world's attacks on healthcare professionals and settings took place in Syria, the remaining one third being spread across the rest of the globe. It also stated that around two thirds of Syria's medical professionals had left the country. Among them were many of the best doctors.

The WHO figures stated that almost 60% of hospitals had either closed or been destroyed or were largely dysfunctional because of the lack of appropriate staff and resources. Many private hospitals closed when their owners fled to safer cities or countries. As doctors were perceived as being well off, they were among those often targeted for kidnapping. Crippling ransoms would be demanded by the gangs and armed groups that took them. The lucky ones would be released on handover of the cash, but others were never seen again.

No one knew what happened to them. Most were assumed dead, but there were also stories of doctors who had been taken and forced to work for armed militias. If sent to the front lines, only the strongest would survive. I talked with one doctor who had managed to escape from one of these groups. He told me how they repeatedly offered him drugs, money and women to encourage him to stay.

There was also speculation over bodies found dumped in certain areas of the country with their vital organs removed. With the breakdown of law and order and the rise of gangs and jihadist armies in the peak of the conflict, a black market was believed to have developed for human organs, removed from donors who had not willingly given them. It seemed inconceivable that any qualified doctor would be a willing party to this kind of depraved murder, or to the theft of organs for sale on the black market, yet the removal and handling of such organs required specialist knowledge and skill if the stolen organs were to be successfully sold or transplanted in a new host.

The need for adequate healthcare was everywhere in Syria, especially in areas where hospitals had been destroyed. This need provided the rationale for the first hospital we opened in Syria.

As we were making the final preparations for opening this hospital, Dr A's spirit was positive and his outlook optimistic. He had gone through a tough patch, but God had been healing his heart. There were many setbacks along the way – incidents that could have driven him to despair, given everything he had already been through. Yet with much encouragement from our faithful prayer group, who would regularly send messages for me to pass on to him, he kept moving forward.

After weeks of preparation we opened our first small field hospital. A team was transported in to work for a week, to be replaced the following week by the next team. Extra security had to be arranged to reassure the teams, and I waited for news of some of the first patients. Shortly after the medics started treating the local residents, two men with gunshot wounds were brought in. They had been transported in the back of someone's pick-up truck after being shot in the street. Onlookers had seen what happened and had stopped to help. They had heard rumours that a hospital had recently opened, but had barely dared to believe it. It had taken the truck an hour and a half to reach our hospital.

One of the men had been shot in the chest, and he was dead on arrival. With no first aid en route, he had lost too much blood to survive. Our team carried out emergency surgery on the second man, who had severe abdominal wounds. He was rapidly dying too. The bleeding had to be stopped. The team worked for four hours on his stomach, intestines and ascending colon. He was just twenty-nine, had a wife and two children, and had been walking home from work. The nearest hospital would have been three and a half hours' drive from where he was shot. Had our simple hospital not existed, this man would not have survived; a woman would have lost her husband, and two young children would have lost their father.

This medical team did so much more than simply carry out a job. They went above and beyond the call of duty according to most standards. They went to work in this difficult area at a time when hospitals were often targeted. Many of them had lost friends or colleagues through killings, kidnappings and bombings. There have been so many incidents and attacks, including armed groups entering and taking over hospitals, and on once occasion an alleged suicide bomber stood in the centre of a hospital department before being wrestled to the ground and arrested, as well as car bombs being parked outside hospital entrances before being detonated. There have been countless rocket attacks on hospitals, and more attacks on healthcare professionals and settings than can be listed here. These doctors and nurses have been the unsung heroes in the conflict in Syria.

It wasn't long before our team was dealing with more tragic events. Post ISIS, the ground was littered with landmines. ISIS and other jihadist armies were known for riddling the places they left with explosives aimed at causing maximum fear and loss of lives.

A farmer and his wife, with their five children, had taken in their widowed sister and her two children. While the couple were working on the land, a mine exploded. The father died at the scene. Two of the workers were injured and needed surgery at our hospital. The mother was alive but more severely injured. The team performed a number of operations on her to stop the bleeding and stabilise her condition. She was in our small and basic intensive care unit, but it wasn't enough. She needed a specialist ICU with more advanced equipment, which even the remaining hospitals in the nearest city were unable to provide at the time. Any hospitals there would have incurred a significant cost in treating her, and even if the family had had the ability to pay for her to go to a private hospital, these insti-tutions were still lacking the most specialist equipment. It would also be a life-threatening transfer for someone in her condition, without any guarantee of the care she could receive or of the outcome once she was there.

The main hospitals which used to provide free care had been destroyed or damaged. The health ministry had attempted to reinstate some of what had been lost, but in smaller buildings and medical centres. But the hospitals that had provided hundreds of beds and many specialist departments and diagnostic services before the war could not be shoehorned into infinitely smaller buildings without the necessary space, equipment, services and staff.

This mother was dying, but she might have had a chance if there had been better resources and an experienced specialist ICU team offering free care, but there wasn't. One night I wept as I processed this situation. Five children had just lost their father, and their mother was deteriorating, having now developed disseminated intravascular coagulation, a condition that was the result of the extensive loss of blood, and that would shortly take her life. She would leave behind five orphans and a widowed sister who was already struggling to support her two children. This widow had been relying on these relatives for her survival. She would now be left caring for seven children, five of whom had lost both their mother and their father. I could barely imagine how they would cope, emotionally or physically.

Over the course of 2016, our humble field hospital treated a growing number of cases as more families returned, and as more people outside the city got word of its existence. In the second half of the year the numbers settled at around 1,000 cases per month.

How to provide meaningful help to the civilians who got caught up in the fighting, while keeping the team and hospital safe was a continuing challenge. Striking a balance between being close enough to the battles to be accessible to those injured, yet not putting a medical team or building in the firing line was a struggle. No one could predict what would change after one month, or after two or three. Some attacks came as a surprise, while other battles could be seen getting closer. We converted a twenty-foot shipping container bought locally into an operating room which could be moved from one location to another.

We started making plans to open another field hospital in another area in need. Although not as far from the nearest city, the connecting road to the city was often too dangerous to traverse as it was targeted by snipers and kidnappers. People could not travel to and from that area after dark, and people died because they could not access emergency medical care. We bought the basic equipment needed for a small field hospital there in August 2016.

When we opened our first field hospital, I remember talking to one of our collectors about our goal of raising £20,000 per month in standing orders. The lady said to me with an encouraging smile that I now needed to employ a fundraiser. But this idea didn't feel right to me. Since my first appeal in 2014, I had depended on God to provide everything, and he had graciously done this. I felt that paying someone to take on a role like this did not reflect the ethos of our work. While I would welcome someone who was willing to help us with this on a voluntary basis, I definitely didn't want to employ someone. I recall saying, 'Where is the opportunity for God to work a miracle if we pay someone to do the fundraising for us?'

In the autumn of 2016 we had reached an amazing regular amount of around £6,000 of the £20,000 per month in standing orders we were aiming for. It was wonderful we had raised this much, but I was hoping for more and felt we had become stuck at this amount. I didn't want to keep asking the same people for money. I had never wanted to pressure people. I felt giving should be encouraged, but should also be spontaneous and something people could do with joy and willingness.

I had done everything I could to raise the money, but it clearly wasn't anywhere near enough. I couldn't do it myself. One day, I stopped for the first time to say a truly heartfelt prayer for the money. Of course, I had asked God before, but on this day there was something different. Where else could we look for a sum like £14,000 per month to come from? I had no idea. We needed a miracle to even come close to this. I also had a strange question in my mind, wondering why God would provide in this way for me or my project. Perhaps he had had enough of working with me? Maybe I was not holy enough to be given this kind of privilege again? Yet somehow I learnt at this time that that is precisely the point.

God does not choose us or give us the privilege of his love, or of his provision for our ministry serving people because we are good, or the best or the most holy. Nor does he demonstrate his power through us because we deserve to be used by him in an amazing way. He works with us and blesses us simply because of his grace and because it is his work we are doing, and because it is him we are serving.

When God sent Jesus to die for each of us, he did it because of his great mercy towards us. When Jesus paid the price for our mistakes, taking the punishment which each of us deserves because we fall short of the perfection he originally intended for us at creation, we did not deserve this gift. He did not give us this precious gift of life because we were good or because we did anything to earn it, or even because we asked for it, as most of us didn't. He did it simply because of his love for us, and because of his grace. His compassion and his kindness to us do not switch off when we make mistakes or when we are far from perfection. When we turn to him in our weakness, acknowledging our faults and limitations with a repentant heart, and accept his gift of love and forgiveness, this is when his grace comes into full effect.

Feeling conscious of my own weakness, I told God that I had done everything I felt I could do without dropping all of the rest of our work, but that I had reached the end of those whom I felt I could ask without feeling I was hassling people. I told him I felt we needed some generous donors to help us with this extra money, and asked him to provide them because I couldn't. I was on my knees.

A couple of weeks later, I went to pick up my son from school. I was chatting to one of the dads who was always friendly and unassuming. He said he had heard about the work I was doing and asked if there was anything he could do to help. Over these years I have had so many offers of help. Many are well-meaning but amount to nothing; some translate into help for a while, then the interest starts to fade. A few translate into true, meaningful and lasting help, but I never know what to expect when people initially offer.

Fundraising was at the forefront of my mind, and I asked him whether he might be interested in helping raise some money for our hospital. I hoped that perhaps he might have business contacts or connections who could support the project a little. He suggested we meet with his wife for a coffee. Before this meeting, I wondered whether they were thinking of making a small one-off donation or perhaps a regular donation themselves, or whether he hoped to connect me with someone else. I had no way of knowing.

'How much do you have, and how much do you need?' he asked, as we sat sipping coffee in a busy café near the school.

'We have around £6,000 per month, and we are trying to get to £20,000. We might be closer to £7,000 now, I'm not sure without checking,' I told him.

'I can't make a long-term commitment, but how about I make up the difference for the next year?' came his baffling response.

The look of confusion must have been clear on my face.

'Sorry, what do you mean when you say, "make up the difference"?'

'Well,' he explained carefully, 'you need £14,000 per month, so twelve times £14,000 makes £168,000. I can pay it monthly or as one lump sum. Which would you prefer?'

Perhaps for the first time in my life, I was completely lost for words! Had I heard him correctly? Did this kind of thing really happen? Did people really have such large sums of money to give away in such a relaxed and modest manner in a café in Brighton?

In the middle of the noisy café we were sitting in, my eyes filled with tears. It wasn't long before his wife and I were both reaching for the serviettes which had come with our coffees.

He told me he trusted us to use the money for what we felt was needed most, whether it was in this hospital or for another.

The next day, I emailed him to check I had understood correctly, worried that perhaps I had not. Did he really say £168,000, and could we really claim an extra 25% gift aid on this donation? The whole experience was overwhelming and very humbling, and was further proof for me that the results we achieve in this work are not so much about what I am doing, although this is clearly important too, but more about what God is doing when we make ourselves available to serve him with all our heart.

Having considered the possibility of buying additional equipment and starting a new department at our first field hospital, we felt guided in the current climate to open a couple of smaller hospitals in different locations to provide help across a larger geographical area, rather than focusing everything in one area. It was not long before we discovered how important that decision would be.

9

The Coming Destruction

Evacuating our first field hospital, December 2016

Although the fighting near our first field hospital continued, the area itself had remained relatively stable since the hospital opened in May 2016. There was military protection around the area, and the team felt comparatively safe. But several months later, the situation changed dramatically.

I had gone on holiday with my family. I had been working flat out over the preceding couple of years, I was feeling tired, and my husband had wanted us to take a family holiday. Part of me felt that going on holiday was not a big priority given this crisis in Syria and with so much poverty in the world, but he was keen to go, and I needed a rest. I had made the decision that I would not let my work take up my time on this holiday as my husband and children had been very understanding about it over the previous couple of years. I wanted to give them some quality time.

When we arrived at our destination, I switched on my phone and saw a message from Dr A. He told me there had been some of the heaviest attacks on the area around our hospital since it had been freed from ISIS earlier in the year. The attacks from ISIS seemed to be under control, but he was asking us to pray for the team there. They had been dealing with a lot of injuries as a result of these attacks.

The next day, I received another message from Dr A asking people in our prayer group to pray for the team in our hospital because the area was under heavy attack again. There were rumours that the area would be taken by ISIS again, and that it could happen soon. This seemed questionable as there had been a heavy military presence better equipped than ISIS guarding the area. ISIS recapturing the area seemed a strange prospect.

It was hard for any of us to know what to do. Our medical team were not from the area, but were driven in each week and driven out again at the end of the week, when a new team was sent in. The team members were our responsibility, as it wasn't as though they were living in their home environment and able to make their own decisions. They were dependent on our management for their safety and their transport out. Some of them there were scared and wanted to leave, but others there were adamant that they wanted to stay. A lot of people were being injured in these attacks. It was very hard for these medical professionals to leave the growing number of casualties behind with no medical support at all within a two-hour radius. Our hospital was the only hope for these injured people. The team carried a huge responsibility, and making these kind of life-or-death decisions on their behalf was an enormous weight for Dr A, and for me.

I was feeling very uneasy, and I had a growing burden to pray for the team there. I felt I couldn't think about or focus on anything other than the need to pray right there and then. I was praying in everything I was doing, but felt an increasing weight and need to focus more and pray more intensely, on my knees, and to be alone with God.

When it was time to go for lunch, I felt extremely uncomfortable. I felt I should fast and pray instead. But I also felt awkward as this was our family time together, and we had only just arrived. It felt difficult to explain to my family and then remove myself from them at a time when we would normally have sat down and eaten together on the first day of our holiday. I knew my husband had been looking forward to us having some time away together as a family, without any work interruptions, and I really wanted all of them to feel I had been present during this holiday. But with every step I took as I walked down to the restaurant, I felt more uncomfortable and my heart heavier. As we reached the restaurant, I couldn't bear it any longer and apologised to my poor husband, telling him I couldn't eat and needed to be alone.

When I got back to the hotel room, I felt I needed to get on my knees and close my eyes to pray. I don't recall ever having felt such an intense and overwhelming burden to pray as I felt at that time. There are times when I find it hard to concentrate on praying even for five minutes, but right then I couldn't think about anything else, I was just completely focused on praying.

After a few minutes, I picked up my Bible and asked God for guidance. I was completely at a loss as to what to do. I asked him to show me by giving me a passage with some relevance to this situation. I closed my eyes and opened the Bible completely at random. With my eyes still closed, I put my fingers randomly between the pages. When I opened the Bible, and then my eyes, the passage I had landed on was 2 Kings 25:8–21. It described the Babylonian invasion of Jerusalem, how the Temple of the Lord was burned down, and how everything was destroyed by the Babylonians, who took some of the priests and put them to death before taking the Israelites into exile.

If I had had the time to sit and analyse it, I might have dealt with the situation differently. But in the heat of the moment, this felt to me like a very clear symbolic warning of something bad coming. It felt like a message from God indicating that the team should leave straight away. I photographed the passage and messaged it to Dr A immediately, telling him my interpretation of it: the Babylonians represented ISIS – evil in God's eyes; Jerusalem represented this area that ISIS were trying to take; and the Temple of the Lord represented our hospital.

I told Dr A I thought the team should leave, and said I was praying they could get out in time. I didn't stop to rationalise, I just followed the very intense feeling I had in my heart that this was God's Word and guidance for us in this situation now. I don't know why we kept messaging rather than picking up the phone to talk – I think I was still in the attitude of prayer.

Dr A didn't question anything, he just messaged back saying OK. Over the last year we had developed a strong trust and understanding of each other's faith. During the course of the conflict in Syria, he had lost a number of hospitals, and some of his doctors and nurses had also been killed. Those experiences had been extremely painful for him, and he wasn't prepared to take a chance with anyone's life while ISIS were attacking.

Four minutes later he messaged me saying the whole team, including the doctors and nurses who had wanted to stay, had left the hospital and were on the road. He had told them to leave everything, to take any patients who wanted to go too, and to leave immediately. I breathed a sigh of relief. He asked me to pray for them as they travelled, as the road was extremely dangerous. ISIS were in and around the area and the team were very exposed as they travelled in vehicles along the lonely road.

I immediately started to feel anxious, as I began to worry that perhaps I had just sent them all to their deaths. What if they were all killed on the road? It was a very real risk as ISIS often put snipers along that road, and sometimes blocked it off, killing people who tried to pass. There were many kilometres they had to pass, and if ISIS were attacking the city, they might also attack or close the road. Either way, they would surely be killed if they were seen. I suddenly started to worry about whether I had made the right decision as I had responded so quickly without analysing my interpretation of the biblical passage I had just read. I had just felt so strongly in my heart that this was what we must do, and I felt a real sense of urgency about it.

Night was falling, and it was December, so the sun set early. This area is a couple of hours' drive from the nearest city, and the road was rough. It was a cloudy night with no lighting along the way. Soon it was getting dark, but the team had no choice but to drive their van and two cars with the lights switched off or risk being seen and killed. It was an impossible scenario.

As they drove, some of the team were very emotional. It was a terrifying experience for them, and also heartbreaking for them to abandon this hospital they had worked so hard to build up and develop over the months. Even though it was so basic on many levels, they were proud of it and, more importantly, of what they were doing there.

Dr A and I were praying for them so intensely, knowing how dangerous the road was. I could not do anything other than pray. As I panicked, I felt the Holy Spirit directing me to worship God while praying, to praise God; the Father, Son and Holy Spirit. For the next half an hour or so, I just felt there was something vitally important about worshipping, and affirming the Holy Trinity; the Father, Son and Holy Spirit, was essential in this. I had heard it said before that worshipping God is the best defence against evil, but in that moment, I actually felt called to live this.

We were praying the team would be kept out of the sight of the ISIS fighters, who were killing people, and that God would guide and protect them. The team could see that other people had been killed and other cars destroyed as they drove along this road.

Around half an hour after our team passed along this most dangerous part of the road, we heard news that it was blocked off completely by ISIS. No one else could leave the area. If they had delayed leaving, even just by half an hour or perhaps even less, they would not have been able to pass at all. They would have been trapped, and unable to leave. They would not have survived.

I can't really explain it, but during the time I had started feeling such a heavy weight to pray, I felt I could not focus on anything other than praying and listening to God. I prayed, read passages from the Bible, sent prayers and passages from the Bible to Dr A and sought God's protection and guidance for the team. Sometime later, I suddenly felt that the weight had been lifted. Something shifted, and I felt as though this intense need to pray had passed.

By now, I felt I could open my eyes and think again. It is hard to explain, but I almost felt as though I had been some-where else, and that at this moment I returned to normality. It was a little like being in labour, without the physical pain, just being absorbed in a different space.

I sent Dr A a message asking if it was appropriate to talk. He said yes. Then he messaged again to say the team had passed through the dangerous area and were finally somewhere safe.

When the team arrived at our other hospital, they told

Dr A they had no idea how they had managed to get there. The road was too dark for anyone to see properly, and they could see that other people and vehicles had been attacked on the way.

We left the hospital to the fate of ISIS or anyone else in the area who might loot it. When the team arrived at the safe hospital, I kept wondering whether my warning them to leave the other one had been a false alarm. Would everything in fact turn out to have been OK there? Had we evacuated it on the spur of the moment and risked the lives of the team unnecessarily? Would lives have been lost which might have been saved if our team had stayed there? Would the team return in a few days after ISIS had been defeated to find the hospital looted and all the equipment gone?

It was a strange situation, and it shouldn't have been possible for ISIS to take that location so quickly. It seemed unbelievable to the people there that it could happen. But God had seen what we couldn't. Within a couple of hours, I saw on the news that ISIS had taken this area completely. There would have been no hope for our team if they had stayed.

Although we lost a hospital that day, I felt an overwhelming sense of peace and assurance, and even victory, because God had clearly been in control of what happened to our team. He had led them through a situation which could have ended very badly for them. Equipment and buildings are replaceable; people are not. I felt so relieved that I had been willing to change my initial decision not to work on this holiday, and had been willing to make myself available to listen to God and respond to him that day. I was also grateful Dr A had been so responsive.

Some months later, when ISIS were forced back out of this place, we sent a team to assess the damage. There was no big structural damage, but there was a lot of superficial damage to the walls. The contents, including the furniture and whatever equipment they didn't steal, had been completely turned upside down and vandalised. ISIS logos and graffiti were painted on the walls in Arabic, saying:

The Islamic State
No God except Allah
And Mohammed is his messenger

It was hard for me to see the photos of what they had done to our little hospital. It must have been harder still for the team who had been working there before. Yet I felt so grateful that the most important element had been protected – our people.

I believe that in situations where people are serving humanity and God, and especially serving the poor and vulnerable, which we were doing there, God is especially present and active. The situation we were faced with that day was life or death, and I believe this is the reason God intervened and guided us in such a clear and dramatic way.

Once again, I saw a clear demonstration of 2 Corinthians 12:9, where Paul learns that God's 'power is made perfect in [our] weakness'. It is not because of our strength or ability that any of these amazing things happen – it is quite the opposite. God's power works best in our weakness and when we depend on him completely, with childlike trust and faith. When he is our only hope and we depend on him, his grace and provision are poured out in a powerful way.

10

Crossing into Syria

Spring 2017

The empty road was in blatant contrast to the busy ones we had navigated just an hour before in Beirut, with their constant flow of cars and hooting horns. There was no sign of another soul on the approach to the border with Syria, except for the car which had just pulled up behind us and into which I would now get. It was time to swap cars. My new driver looked tougher and was less friendly. He had not been employed for his hospitality skills, but rather for his ability to protect and assist at the border.

On the Syrian side I was ushered into the room of the officer in charge. A woman in her forties perched gingerly on the edge of a threadbare seat nestled among the couches lining the walls of the room. It appeared not to have had a change of furniture since the 1970s. I was shown to a seat on the opposite side of the room, and I sat, looking first at the long-haired woman in front of me, then to the uniformed man who sat behind the desk.

While he talked on the phone, smoke wafted from the cigarette resting in an ashtray on his desk. After some time, he addressed the woman, whose face broke into a smile and she suddenly looked more relaxed. She took back her passport and another piece of paper, and was then escorted from the room. Another man in a different uniform handed the officer at the desk the packet of documents our Syrian team had prepared to support my request for a visa. The officer's next phone call was more animated and emotional. In spite of my poor Arabic, the one thing I was sure of was that he was unimpressed by my British passport. I heard him mention it a number of times, sounding less enthusiastic on each occasion. I began to feel a little apprehensive; after all, there were no guarantees he would grant me a visa. It occurred to me that it was time to start praying.

A couple of minutes later, the uniformed man who had just handed over my supporting documents returned with a mobile phone, which he politely offered to the officer behind the desk.

'Dr A,' he said as he handed the phone to his superior. My ears pricked up, and my eyes followed each of the men closely. I began to pray harder. This would be a pivotal conversation.

They talked for a few minutes, the officer taking the packet of documents and scanning through some of them, with the phone sandwiched between his ear and his shoulder. After a few minutes, the call ended. For the first time, the officer turned to me and looked me in the eye.

'Welcome to Syria,' he said respectfully, in English.

My shoulders relaxed, and he asked where I was planning on staying for this trip. We talked for a few moments before he looked me intently in the eye again. Then he said, with genuine gratitude, 'Really, I want to thank you for everything you are doing for us.'

My heart skipped a beat as, with the stamp in my passport, we drove off from the border. I could barely believe I was finally in Syria. I motioned to the driver, asking if it was OK to take photos as we drove along. 'No' was his blunt reply. Following another car and driver change for additional security, I was met by Haitham, a Syrian Christian who would travel around much of Syria with me.

Haitham had been severely injured during the height of the conflict. A terrorist had planted a bomb in his car a few years before, just weeks before his wedding. Haitham was an ordinary citizen, an employee in an insurance company at that time, with no political agenda.

Both of his legs were severely injured in the explosion. People ran to his rescue, and with little hope of an ambulance, they laid him across the back seat of a taxi. His bloody, mangled legs were put through the open window as there was nowhere else to put them.

He arrived at the public hospital with huge chunks of flesh burnt and blown off his legs, but they did not initially accept him; they were unable to cope. However, the people who had taken him there argued with the hospital staff and they eventually began treating him. Haitham's employer fortunately arranged healthcare and he was moved to a private hospital where he received long-term treatment.

He needed numerous operations both at the time and over the next couple of years. Large parts of the flesh from his leg are missing. It took him weeks to learn to walk again. Amazingly, his wedding went ahead as planned and he was able to walk down the aisle.

After this senseless attack, the man who had planted this bomb was caught and prosecuted. He didn't know Haitham, and Haitham didn't know him. When he was asked in court why he carried out this attack, he replied, 'I wanted to create fear and make people feel unsafe.' He achieved his aim.

Haitham is both a victim of the crisis in Syria but also part of the solution. This is true of most people who have worked with our team in Syria. Every one of them has many terrifying and heartbreaking stories of family members, friends, neighbours and colleagues being kidnapped, killed or injured. What moves me most is to see their courage and inner strength. The Syrian people are so genuine and so beautiful. They don't deserve what they have suffered for so many years.

After Haitham's initial treatment he was left with shrapnel in his leg which, a couple of years later, became painful, inflamed and swollen, and he spiked a temperature of 40°C. When he went to a different public hospital – one which I later visited with him – the doctor he saw there said there was no one to do an X-ray of his leg, so he should come back the next day. But even Haitham knew he needed some kind of treatment immediately. He left the hospital, and one of the doctors working with our team treated him with the antibiotics he needed. He also needed surgery to remove the abscesses which had developed around the shrapnel still embedded in his leg. In the end, this too was organised by one of the doctors from our team.

People's expectations of the medical system in Syria have sunk very low. Healthcare is now a luxury, and today many people die from conditions that were treated easily before the war. Yet it is a miracle that they are able to provide any kind of service at all, after so many years of brutal conflict and sanctions that have made it so difficult for healthcare providers to import life-saving equipment and medications. The cascade of negative effects go so much deeper. Yet the people living in these areas with functioning public hospitals, which are working hard and struggling to provide a service in such difficult circumstances, consider themselves to be very blessed in comparison with those who have lived in areas under siege, where the situations were far worse.

After arriving at the hotel where I spent my first night, I waited with Haitham for Dr A. After working so closely with Dr A, it was a blessing to finally meet him. I had brought with me the Bible that he had requested the year before, when he had asked for 'the same English Bible that one of our prayer team had used'. I had attempted to post my Bible to him the year before using a special international postal service. Months passed and nothing arrived in Syria. I felt disappointed, as that particular Bible had been to many places with me, and I had underlined meaningful passages in it. Nine months after I had posted it, it was returned through my letterbox in the UK! By then I was planning my first trip to Syria, and it was a great honour to be able to finally hand it to Dr A in person. We had much to discuss and plan for my time there, so we prayed and read certain passages from his new Bible. We didn't map out my time there, but rather prayed and were led by God as to where to visit, and on which days.

I will never forget the first displaced widow and mother of five I met in Draikeesh. She and her children had fled from Aleppo. She described how 'the terrorists', as she and the other people I met called them, had come and set fire to their home. But the loss she could never recover from was of her thirteen-year-old daughter, who those fighters took when they captured the neighbourhood. Now living in a tiny, unfurnished building with no kitchen, and with five other families sharing the same space, she showed me a photo of her stunningly beautiful girl who she had not seen since that day, three years before.

For the sake of her other children, she had been forced to flee without her precious daughter. As I looked at the picture showing her daughter's beautiful long black hair, I couldn't fight back my own tears. It was clear why they had taken her. I wept with this woman, hugging her as she squeezed her eyes together trying to shut out the pain. I struggled, swallowing my tears and trying to regain my composure for her sake.

Everyone across Syria knows what those fighters do to the girls they take. I could hardly bear to imagine what this poor woman had been through since that day, in torment as she wondered whether her daughter was still alive, and if she was, what kind of ordeal she was forced to endure each day.

The kidnapped girl's younger sister stood next to us, silently wiping away her tears. The impact of these cruel events affects everyone in a family, and I didn't know how this grieving widow could even begin to explain to her younger daughter what had happened to her big sister, or why. How can anyone explain the inexplicable? There must have been days when this mother wondered in her heart whether it would be better for her daughter to be dead. I felt I had shared a piece of this widow's heart that day. She was so gentle, and she possessed a simple innocence, being so trusting and open about her experiences, feelings and emotions.

At the time of writing there are still schools, sports complexes and public buildings across Syria being used to accommodate families who fled, just as this family did, when armed extremists took the areas in which they were living. Often between twenty and forty families would be squeezed into one school building. I visited some of these buildings, and met family after family as I went from room to room, speaking with each one. They all told similar stories, many having come from the same areas. They had been attacked in their homes and neighbourhoods by armed Islamist groups – Jabhat al-Nusra, the Free Syrian Army and ISIS were some of the names I heard repeatedly and most frequently from the displaced people I met in different locations across Syria.

I also visited some of these areas after the sieges were broken. The tragic stories we heard from the ordinary people who had lived through the sieges were heart-wrenching.

Members of one displaced family I met in a safer part of Syria were living in a makeshift hut they had constructed from pieces of plastic, metal, scaffolding and wood. They told me how they had fled from Idlib in the north of Syria when armed groups took their neighbourhood by force. I asked the parents about the rest of their family as not all of their children were with them. They told me their oldest children were still in Idlib. At that time, I had been puzzled as to why they had stayed when their parents had left. With ashen faces and downcast eyes, the mother said wretchedly that the jihadists now controlling the area killed everyone who tried to leave, so they were trapped there. They managed to talk with them occasionally on the phone, but life was very difficult, dangerous and scary for the people who had not managed to get out in time. They were the human shields of the groups controlling the area.

It was disturbing hearing the displaced people's unbearable accounts of when they were first attacked, as well as those of the people who had continued to live in those areas while under siege and also when the sieges were being broken. I had not heard all of these stories in England. Everywhere I travelled in Syria the stories were of similar ferocious cruelties and slaughter, committed by armed extremists on an enormous scale against ordinary people in their neighbourhoods, in their homes and sometimes in their own beds. It was hard to believe that such things could be taking place here in Syria, and, from these people's reports, on such a huge scale, while the rest of the world was told little or nothing about them.

In one city I visited a widow who had fled Aleppo with her family when armed jihadists arrived and started killing people in their neighbourhood, and then took their home. Tragically, her husband had died sometime before. She had six children. Two of her daughters were severely disabled, needing full care and unable to walk. The family were living in an unfinished building with no windows and bare breeze-block walls. Their empty and comfortless home was like a building site.

In spite of the immense traumas this family had suffered and the huge burdens they had been carrying, this woman's oldest son had managed to keep his focus, and won a scholarship to medical school. As well as studying full time to become a doctor, he worked in the evenings to support his mother and siblings. For this family, he was their only hope for the present and the future. Once qualified, he would carry a heavy responsibility for caring for his family for the foreseeable future.

As well as giving them some clothes, we gave them a wheel-chair so that the girls could sometimes leave the house. When we asked what his sisters needed, the young man humbly asked just for incontinence pads. He didn't like to ask for more.

A year later I visited them again. I explained that we didn't have a lot, but would give what we could. As I was leaving to go and collect the things they needed, the young man approached me and said, 'It doesn't matter whether you give us something big or small, what matters is you have been thinking of us and you care. You have taken the time to come back here to us. You remembered us. This means more to us than anything you give us.' This really touched my heart.

As we left, we felt that we would really like to do something for the youngest girl as it was her birthday that day. When we returned with the items we had picked up for them, we also took some hot food and a big chocolate birthday cake. The smiles on their faces as we sang happy birthday were heart-warming.

It was really special spending the evening with this family. As they were a Muslim family, Haitham sat in a separate room with the widow's brother-in-law, while I ate with the women and children. By this time, I had been able to learn a little Syrian Arabic. Although I still had a long, long way to go, it was nice to be able to communicate with them just a little without someone translating for me.

Often our gestures, whether large or small, mean more to people than the size of our gifts for them. Many people are not in a position to give a lot, but if we each give a little, we can lift the hearts and spirits of these people who have lost everything. The worst thing for anyone is to feel forgotten or abandoned. It makes a person feel insignificant and worthless. But to know you have been remembered makes you feel like a valued human again, and that your life matters.

II

Aleppo: Syria's Second Largest City

Spring 2017

The road to Aleppo offered some indication of what lay ahead. But nothing could prepare me for the scale and intensity of the destruction I found in the city itself.

On both sides of the long desert road, remains of entire villages lay abandoned. Piles of debris and the crumbling ruins of homes cluttered the edges of the road, which stretched many kilometres. Remnants of hand-crafted mud houses with perfectly rounded roofs provided evidence of how some of the simplest communities had lived before the war. Yet even these villages had not been spared. All were deserted, and many lay in pieces. If this was what was left of the homes, my heart tightened as I thought about what might have become of the inhabitants.

At intervals along the road, large banks of sand had been formed into raised protective circles which allowed soldiers to keep watch without exposing themselves to obvious danger. Some were big, and some were especially creative, using old tyres, empty oil barrels and blocks, which added extra features to these sentry points.

The road signs leading into the city were punctured with bullet holes. I could barely imagine the ferocity of the battle that must have taken place there in the middle of this wide road to leave even the road signs looking battered.

A lone man wheeled a laden bicycle through a cloud of dust that filled the avenue as we approached Old Aleppo. We drove through street after street after street of rubble and desecrated buildings. I could hardly take in the sheer volume of the destruction, which was breath-taking in its immensity and awfulness. We passed through scores of streets in which every remaining building was stamped with the ragged, characteristic trademarks of this merciless war.

There are no words to adequately describe the nature or extent of the devastation in that part of Aleppo. It was a post-apocalyptic scene, where no building lay unscathed, and where damaged structures towered on either side of the rubble-lined roads. These were once some of the busiest districts of Syria's trade and industrial capital, but on the day we visited, the silence of these now desolate streets lined with buildings that were little more than windowless skeletons was interrupted only by the sound of our car. As we stopped to survey the destruction, a solitary figure clad from head to foot in a black abaya walked quickly through the deserted street. What business could she possibly have here, I wondered, in a place so barren and uninhabited? It was impossible to imagine these buildings being used for anything now. Surely they were all uninhabited? Or were they?

As I surveyed these mind-blowing scenes, the most stunning realisation was that we had created this. Us. The human race. Looking at each ruin, I began to calculate the magnitude of time, money, planning and human passion which had been invested in creating this level of destruction. Wow. If I hadn't seen, felt, smelled and tasted this devastation towering over me, I could never have believed it could be real, or that humanity was capable of it.

To build anything – a house, an office block, a school, a hospital – takes years of raising the money to build it, planning it, designing it and watching it slowly develop. But more important are the hopes, the creativity, the enthusiasm and the commitment which go hand in hand with making these dreams come true. Yet in a matter of moments, all of these can be shattered. Not just the buildings, but the hopes, dreams and creations of our fellow humans. Their lives had been torn apart. Their dreams had been ripped away, their hopes had been broken and their creations had been destroyed. May God forgive us all for our part in allowing this, whether we realise our responsibility or not.

We parked near the citadel, in what was once the vibrant and diverse tourist hub of the city. Neama was a Syrian Christian, as well as my host, and I would get to know her better over the next few days. She pointed to an expanse of rubble which had been a hotel. A few people milled around near the approach to the citadel, posing for photos in front of the sign which read 'Believe in Aleppo'.

Many government buildings in what was now a large open area with mounds of misshapen stones had met the same fate. A burnt-out covered souk, previously a thriving traditional market, was now forsaken and filled with debris. Thick black soot on the ceiling displayed scrapings etched by errant bullets, exposing the pale stone behind. The light was fading as evening began to draw in.

The eerie silence of this tomb-like expanse was broken suddenly by the piercing sound of gunfire. The distinctive sound of a machine gun echoed off the broken stones and I looked immediately to Neama. She continued talking without even blinking, so I scanned each of my other companions for their reaction. Their indifference told me this was a familiar sound to them. I assured myself that if it wasn't troubling these locals, I would be fine, too, if I kept close and remained alert.

As we drove towards the thriving western part of the city, a raised patch of grass, previously a small park, was pointed out. It now exhibited a multitude of gravestones. Myriads of electricity cables were networked between the buildings on both sides of each road, creating a valuable web providing power for the city. But it was only available at certain hours of the day, when residents would charge their phones and batteries, ready for the next absence of power.

That evening, Neama took me to the apartment where she lived with her sister Nahla. The two front rooms of the small flat were empty. She explained how the glass in their windows had been blown out so many times that they had given up replacing it. She delicately touched the plastic they had used in place of the glass as she explained how they had moved their living area to the windowless corridor leading from the front door to the other rooms of the apartment. It hadn't been safe to sleep in the front bedrooms.

The sweet smell of traditional Arabic tobacco drifted in as Nahla sat on the balcony smoking a sheesha pipe. She was suffering from depression, having recently suffered significant personal bereavement. Through a weary smile she pointed directly below her seat on the balcony, indicating the place where a bomb had exploded in the road just months before. As I peered over the edge of the balcony, I could see a small crater remaining in the surface of the road. This had been one of many rockets that had hit their residential street. The sisters said they could tell where the rockets came from because of the direction they were travelling from: east Aleppo. The siege there had finally been broken after an intense bombing campaign just four months before. The fighters, their families and their supporters had been evacuated out to Idlib in December. Subsequently, the continuous barrage of rockets which had become part of daily life there, and in the rest of Aleppo, had finally stopped. The next day we would be visiting some of the orphans and widows in east Aleppo who had lost everything.

The three of us slept in that corridor, where they had built a partition to afford some level of privacy for the only bed. In line with Syrian hospitality, each sister took a couch for the duration of my visit. I lay on the only bed in the darkness listening to the sound of explosions, which I had been assured were in the distance. Yet I couldn't help feeling a knot in my stomach with each blast. This area was the safest it had been in years, but the sound of safety for me was complete silence, whereas our team here were now grateful if the sound of explosions was in the distance.

Over the previous days, I had been taking aid to families in a variety of settings in other parts of Syria. They had fled from Aleppo and its surrounding areas when the problems started. They could be found in every city, in all manner of places, including unfinished buildings, schools and other public buildings, as well as in cobbled-together tent-like structures by the roadside in rural areas.

A few days before, I met most of the twenty-eight families housed in a school. Earlier in the year the building had been infested with rats, and they had also had a hepatitis A outbreak. In one dank, bare room lived an old man from Aleppo with his wife and son. Before the war, he had a high standard of living. He had been a businessman and had owned some shops and a small factory for making and repairing shoes. The terrorists, as he described them, took everything from him – his shops, his factory and their home.

He told me how he, his wife and his son had been kidnapped by them and kept imprisoned in one room for three months. He described how one day, when there was a large attack on that armed group, the three of them found an opportunity to escape, knowing that one wrong move could cost them their lives.

The people I met talked about countless evil acts committed against the ordinary people in their neighbourhoods. People were deliberately targeted and killed for no reason other than that they didn't agree with the radical Islamist ideology of these groups that took their areas. Many who didn't escape in time were not allowed to leave. These people's continuing presence there made it much harder for retaliatory attacks to be carried out, in an effort to return these homes and businesses to their original owners.

I wept with these traumatised people as they broke down, while relating their harrowing accounts. Some reported having been given contaminated fuel by the new controlling groups – fuel which exploded when they tried to use it, injuring those in the direct vicinity. Mothers talked about their teenage daughters having been taken by the fighters and not knowing what had become of them. There were many widows whose husbands had been killed or who disappeared and were assumed dead, and who now struggled to earn a pittance, while their neighbours cared for their young children.

Some people described how, at first, some of these armed groups lulled people into a false sense of security when they arrived, reassuring them and giving them the impression that they were good, and that they wouldn't hurt them. Then, very suddenly, they started killing and abusing anyone who didn't support them.

The story of the old man from Aleppo moved me as I tried to imagine how terrifying the experience he went through must have been for him, and for his wife, but especially for his son, who was just six years old at the time. How could they begin to explain this ordeal to their son at this tender young age? But what moved me most was that when I was walking back to the car with our team, he approached me. He had been waiting there for us with something on his mind. He first thanked me graciously for everything we had been doing and told me he felt that English people must be very kind. 'But,' he went on, 'why do your people support the terrorists?'

This was an uncomfortable, hard-hitting question for me. I had seen articles claiming that western governments, and also some charities, had provided support for some of the jihadist groups and those linked with them, whether directly or indirectly. But this information is not easy to find, or to verify, in the UK. This man had lost everything he had worked so hard for all his life, and had been reduced to living in one room of a dirty, rat-infested school with many other families, and without the ability to provide enough food for his own. They had no home. He had lost his past, he had no future and it would be hard to describe him as even having a present, as no one would choose this kind of existence. His is just one story among millions.

I explained how it is so difficult for people in the UK to understand what has happened in Syria. I apologised to him for everything he had suffered, and told him we would continue to pray for the truth to be understood, and that he and his people would have peace in their country again.

Neama and I were preparing to go and visit some orphans and widows in Hanano in east Aleppo. The taxi had been arranged beforehand, with the regular driver who assisted her with all the aid distributions. But in the morning, when the driver saw me with my pale freckly skin and blue eyes, he lost his nerve. Taking a British person into this sensitive area that was still under strict military control was not an attractive prospect for any ordinary Syrian. This sweet man was a simple driver who had already seen his precious son killed in this war. He had lost enough. Our team might trust me, but why should he? Who was I, what was my business there, why was I going into this sensitive zone which was still under military protection? The UK was one of Syria's enemies, so how could he be sure I wasn't connected to an outside intelligence agency working against them?

Neama had been negotiating with her taxi driver for about half an hour before I realised that I was the problem. It took an hour for her to persuade him to take me, and I felt more and more uncomfortable as this negotiation continued. If it hadn't been for him trusting her, I wouldn't have made it there. In such a politically complex war zone as Syria, ordinary people live in fear of so many basic things most English people would not even blink at. In this messy war, no one wanted to put themselves in a situation where they would end up being questioned, and certainly not for aiding someone from a western country who could have a more sinister motive for being there, using humanitarian aid as a cover. Even between many Syrian people, trust was at an all-time low. But for foreigners, especially from a nation associated with the war in Syria, many people didn't trust them at all.

Reluctantly, the driver allowed me into his taxi, and I tried hard to fight back my tears as we drove through the city. Life in Syria is tough for everyone, on so many different levels. Whichever side people sit on, there are limitations, fears and risks. In the end, it is the ordinary and the poorest people who pay the highest price, usually for something they are not guilty of.

As the day went on, the driver warmed to me a little. But each journey involving searching the unnamed streets for the next family was marked by ongoing, sometimes heated disagreements between Neama and him over taking photos and videos. It felt important to show our supporters back home the real situation for people living in this fractured war zone. Nevertheless I had abruptly learnt the intense risks of taking pictures in these restricted, destroyed areas while I had been in Hamadiyah in Homs a few days before. As a result, I always asked my hosts before taking any pictures, and made sure they told me exactly when to stop if they saw a checkpoint or soldier ahead. Everyone in Syria avoids situations in which they may be asked questions. 'Yes, take pictures. It is fine here,' Neama reassured me confidently, just as the driver would yell, 'No photos!', drowning out her voice.

The main roads in Hanano had largely been cleared, with the rubble pushed into huge heaps by the roadsides. In one town square, a huge necropolis of burnt-out vehicle skeletons piled on top of each other gave an indication of the scale of violence people there had lived through daily. A partially destroyed building with ragged blown-out gaps which once held windows overlooked our yellow taxi. I stared in disbelief at a family seated behind one of these blast holes drinking tea.

People holding plastic jerry cans gathered around some of the large red tanks, now the only source of water for those living in this area. The infrastructure had been destroyed while it was under siege. Some of the homes were a long walk from these water tanks, made even more arduous by the blazing sun beating down. We had discovered exactly how long a walk it was as we carried bags of aid through the maze of rubble-filled alleyways, looking for the homes of the orphans we were visiting.

One widowed grandmother cared for her late son's three children. Her son had been killed in the war, and the mother of the children had been pressured by her family to remarry. In these communities, this pressure to remarry sometimes came from the parents of widowed women. For the families I visited, this had meant that the woman not only had to give up her children, but would never see them again. The grandmother told me with tears streaming down her face that the children's mother still lived in Aleppo, but they hadn't heard from her for a couple of years. The old woman was struggling to cope alone and had cropped the hair of all three girls after repeated infestations of headlice. I mistook them for little boys when we arrived as their hair was so short.

As a mother, I struggled to hear these distressing accounts, yet I was to hear many more from families like this. I simply could not believe that this many women would willingly abandon their children, never to see them again, for the sake of marrying a new husband; they must surely have been under an enormous social pressure.

I came across many grandmothers struggling with the burden of raising two, three or more young and energetic grandchildren while being older themselves. But the burden was often even heavier as the widows we helped were usually alone and had no income, no pension, and often very little family support. I wept with them as they poured out their hearts to us.

One grandmother clung on to me, her shoulders shaking, as I hugged her. Our tears flowed together as she told me how her son had been killed and her daughter-in-law had remarried, leaving her, an older widow, to raise her two young granddaughters. The two girls were young enough to remember nothing but war and the sound of bombs in their short little lives. How many nights had they lain awake, unable to sleep because of the explosions which rocked the buildings all around them? What had they thought and felt when the blasts shook their home? The girls had been silently watching me during my visit.

The older of the two girls had never been able to speak, despite being the same age as my talkative eldest child, who was well established in primary school. This widowed grandmother was sure the girl could hear and understand, but her mutism was likely a result of the trauma of life in east Aleppo during the years of the siege, and of the bombs which had become part of life there. We have encountered a number of children like this in Syria. As this woman wiped tears from her eyes, she told us she hoped her granddaughters would grow up to be like us, and thanked me for coming and sharing her pain. It was a candid and humbling experience.

One extended family with nineteen children was living in a tiny collection of rooms with a sheet of corrugated iron as a front door. As my eyes adjusted to the dim light inside the windowless room, I saw a small child sleeping through all the noise on a cushion on the floor. Another small toddler cried relentlessly. Instinctively I picked him up and hugged him to my waist. Immediately he stopped crying, watching me with fascination instead as I smiled at him. After a few moments one of the issues faced by these poorest families became all too obvious to me: the lack of nappies. The toddler's urine-soaked clothes had resulted in a cold, wet patch on my mine.

Two of those nineteen children had been orphaned in the conflict. Their aunt, with her face mostly covered, pointed to a poster on the wall of two soldiers in uniform. Gesturing to the man on the left, she explained that he was the father of her two nephews. She told us he was beheaded by ISIS, and that he died a martyr, as the Syrians call the people whose lives have been taken by this ugly war in Syria. She said the mother of the two boys died of 'sadness' a year later. At the time we visited, the boys were just four and two and a half years old. Would they remember either of their parents? What would life be like for two orphans growing up in poverty in a family of nineteen children?

We also visited four children living with their grandparents. They had been displaced twice but had returned to live in a house near their old damaged apartment which had been hit by a rocket, just a few doors down. Both parents had been killed while going to the market to buy food. The grandmother shed many tears as she told us how she had lost her daughter and son-in-law to a bomb. We hugged and kissed, and she kissed me again and again, grateful to find someone who would ask, who would listen to them, and who cared.

On the morning I left Aleppo, Neama gave one of the most moving interviews I have recorded in Syria. Her emotions were current and raw. She had lived through such suffering. I will never forget her words or her pauses to control her tears, wipe her eyes and catch her breath.

We are kind people. We don't deserve this. We don't deserve to die. Rich or poor, we all went through tough things, saw a lot of death. We saw our friends die, parents die, some saw their children die. Death is everywhere. We lost our friends, families and we lost our normal lives.

When you are woken every day by the sound of war machines, guns and bombs, you get used to hearing those sounds. You start to wonder whether you have lost your humanity. We lost our selves for a while. We lived like we were no one. We were just numbers. You hear on the news, ten died here, ten died there. We feel we are just numbers. Nobody cares.

What can I do? I don't want to leave my home or my country, I don't want to lose my friends or my job. I decided to stay and 'fight'. Everyone who stayed here is a fighter. We tried to make it normal for ourselves, going to work, doing what we used to do before. We go for walks, try to make a life, try to ignore the war. We pretend to live a normal life. We pretend we are living.

We are damaged inside just like the buildings you saw. You can see the stones on the street, you can see the buildings destroyed, but inside every person going through the war: they are more damaged than the buildings. We are burning inside.

Normal life for us is life with fear. Going to work wondering what might happen on the way. Maybe a terrorist will blow himself up next to me, maybe a bomb will explode, or I will be shot.

People go to work and say goodbye to their family each day because they don't know if they will see them again. People kissed their children goodbye and went to work just to earn enough money to eat, but they never went back to their children, they died out there in the street. They died without any reason.

Many nights I couldn't sleep because of the sounds of people shooting each other. One night it was so close we could hear the words they were shouting to each other. It was an awful night. I cried from fear. I was alone, and the bombs were so strong, the whole house was shaking. People called each other, asking should we pack and leave our houses? We didn't know what to do. It was awful.

After 1 a.m., all the people were awake. No one could sleep that night, then a huge rocket hit our houses. Thirty to forty rockets. We couldn't imagine the damage they were doing, but the sound was terrifying. I was crying and didn't know what to do. At 6 a.m. the fighting calmed, and we decided to walk in the street to see what happened.

The building at the end of the street was completely destroyed. We went and saw. Two to three buildings went down. The people were all sleeping, all the families with children were killed. Forty people in our neighbourhood died. We just stood and cried in silence. It was chaos. People were crying and asking for water. Someone was trying to get people out from under the stones. People were covered in dust. It was an unforgettable night. Around 100 people died that night from those rockets.

In my street, we had three bombs and two rockets. One bomb below our balcony. They put small pieces of metal in the bombs so when they exploded, they fire everywhere, hurting many more people.

We are now trying to stand up, trying to live again, to fix our damage inside and outside, trying to hold each other's hands. Lots of people want to help each other. Syrian people are simple, they don't want much in life, just simple things. They want electricity, water to drink and for washing their clothes. It has been so hard to get the basic things in Aleppo.

Maybe one day we can make Aleppo the way it was. It is a wonderful city. I want everyone to come to Aleppo, it is safe now. Come and meet the people we helped. I wish that. We are so thankful for all the work you are doing, you are inspiring people. We don't mean anything to you, yet you still want to help us. I wish you all happiness in your life, and I wish the best for each member of your family.

12

A Doctor Injured, and the Vision for a New Hospital

June 2017

The bad news came while we were talking on the phone. One of Dr A's medical aquaintances had been seriously injured by a landmine that day. The man with him was killed by the explosion, and Dr Bassam was now in a critical condition in intensive care. We didn't know if he would survive. Most of the ICU departments in Syria were lacking vital resources. Many remaining doctors in Syria were inexperienced in the complexities of something as specialist as intensive care.

Dr Bassam quickly deteriorated into multiple organ failure. We were very concerned he would die. Dr A knew the hospital he had been taken to in that area. It wasn't good, yet there wasn't a better hospital he could be moved to. Dr A could see that managing him a different way might have given him a better chance, but it was such a sensitive situation.

'We need a miracle, Samara. I don't think anything else can save him.'

As Dr A's words sank in, I was beside myself as I tried to process the injustice of this horrific situation. I decided to fast and pray for Dr Bassam. What else could we do? We felt so helpless.

After evacuating the field hospital, we had struggled to find a suitable building to use in its place, but we began to speak of this next hospital as Jerusalem (which we soon renamed Grace), as the passage I had been given when asking God for guidance about whether to evacuate our first hospital talked about the Babylonians invading Jerusalem.

Dr A had bought some land in a calm, unaffected area in one

of the cities. We had started to think about building a small hospital there, rather than just putting some of the meditainers we had been making from containers on it, or continuing to look for existing buildings that were far from perfect but that we could use rent-free. As our ideas progressed, so did our ambitions for the little hospital.

The medical system is one of the most significant casualties of the war in Syria, as so many hospitals have been lost, whether they were closed by owners leaving the area or the country, damaged, or completely destroyed. Many have simply been unable to provide an effective service to everyone in need because of the lack of resources and effective management. Many hospital buildings that could have been providing a service if they had the right money, equipment, supplies and management instead stood unused.

We had re-opened a small hospital on a short lease in the Aleppo area which had previously closed. We ran it on a not-for-profit basis, which meant we carried out nearly half of the treatment and operations free of charge for the poorest patients. To finance this, we offered subsidised rates to other NGOs, so that they could offer treatment to more people. We also treated some private patients at low, affordable prices, which generated the funds to run the hospital and cover the costs each month of treating the free patients.

We treated a baby boy who had a large inguinal hernia needing surgery. When his mother took him to the public hospital providing free care in that area, they said they did not have the resources or ability to carry out the operation he needed in the short term.

What really broke my heart was that just three weeks before we operated on this baby, his father had collapsed and died hours after being sent home from the same hospital that was unable to treat his son. He had gone there with chest pain, but was sent home with no investigatory work having been carried out. They were stretched beyond their capacity and did not have the resources or ability to deal with his heart attack.

As a former A&E nurse, I could not fathom how this could

even have been possible. A young man in his thirties, and with a family, going to an emergency department with chest pain needs a full assessment, an ECG, blood tests and observation. After visiting a number of hospitals in Syria and understanding the services offered by many others, I came to understand that many hospitals in Syria simply don't have the specialist cardiac resources to treat someone having a heart attack. I also learnt that many hospitals are afraid of a patient dying in their care, and would sooner send them away than have them die on their premises, when they know they don't have the resources to treat them. They fear the repercussions, yet the circumstances are not their fault. It is a desperately sad situation, most obviously for the patients and community, but also for the doctors and nurses working in those hospitals. They must feel so helpless.

It had been well documented by many official sources that between 300,000 and 600,000 people had been killed in the conflict in Syria. But these figures completely neglected the legions of victims, like this young father, who died simply because they couldn't access medical care for a condition which could potentially have been treated if all the public hospitals had been fully resourced and functioning, as they had been before the war.

These people who died through lack of medical treatment, for diseases that affect every population, are casualties of the Syrian war just as much as anyone killed by a bomb or a gun. When the deaths related to fighting ceased in many areas as they became more peaceful, people still struggled to access medical treatment for many conditions. Before the war, there were public hospitals in every city working to standards, where a Syrian person could receive emergency treatment free of charge. Intensive care in the public hospitals was free too, while some more complex surgeries, such as cardiac surgery, would have been provided at a reduced cost.

The stories of people like this desperately unfortunate father are not isolated accounts. Across Syria there are many people, each with a handful of stories like this, either about themselves or about someone they know, who could not gain appropriate

emergency treatment. Many people in Syria in need of a significant operation or medical treatment would now choose to travel
outside Syria to receive treatment if they had the money and
the ability to both leave the country and return.

Before the war, there were occasions when patients travelled
to Syria for treatment for certain conditions, but now many
Syrians would travel to Lebanon or elsewhere for their hospital
care if they could. However, the majority of people in Syria
have little or no means to travel long distances, and certainly
not to cover the inflated fees needed to pay for their care in a
foreign country.

After making the decision to turn to God for help, some of
us fasted, asking him to have mercy on Dr Bassam and his family.
That afternoon, I started to feel angry. How was it possible for
a doctor, someone who has given so much to his community,
to die like this? Surely a doctor should be able to access the
best medical care? Surely someone providing medical services
could hope for the best treatment available for themselves?

If any of us in the UK ended up in intensive care, we could
be sure we would have the very best care. We would have all
the expensive up-to-date equipment needed, all the medication,
and most of all, we would have staff with the necessary expertise.
British doctors are trained to a high standard and work within
a framework of protocols which can be depended on, and most
importantly, in the UK healthcare is free for all citizens.

I felt something shift in my heart.

'What would it cost to build and equip a hospital where we
could provide an intensive care department we could truly
depend on in a situation like this?' I asked Dr A. 'Somewhere
we would feel we could move someone like Dr Bassam if something like this happened again?'

'I really don't know. Maybe two million dollars? I'm just
guessing, I don't have any figures,' Dr A replied.

'But how much do you think it would cost to build a hospital
with all the right equipment which could be used for training
and developing doctors' skills so they can gain the experience
to provide the best care for ICU patients?' I pushed.

'It is hard to say. Maybe more like six million dollars. We would need to find out.'

'Well,' I thought out loud, 'that is what we should be aiming for. We serve a big God, and nothing is impossible for him. We shouldn't be limited by what we think we can or can't afford, we should aim for what is truly needed.'

There were two plots of land for sale next to the first one which had been bought. We prayed the next day that if God wanted us to build this bigger hospital, the owner would agree to sell these two plots for the money we had available, which was much lower than the original asking price. The owner did agree to our offer, and we bought the land.

We were amazed as Dr Bassam made a remarkable recovery, and was soon discharged from hospital. Over the next year, however, Dr A lost contact with him. Although his body had survived, it was as if his soul had died. The confident, motivated and energetic man had gone. There was little left of the man Dr A had known before.

According to WHO figures, 1.5 million people have been disabled by the war in Syria. How many more people are there in Syria like Dr Bassam, injured, incapacitated and living like someone who has died? People with such severe injuries need healing for their hearts, not just for their bodies. Dr Bassam's injury, however, was the catalyst for our ambitious vision to design and build a bigger, better hospital which could be a true light in this damaged land. We began to dream a bigger dream than I had ever imagined I could dream.

But the more ambitious this project became, the more sure I was that this was God's vision, not just ours. I am convinced we should dream big dreams for ending poverty, caring for the sick and reaching out to the vulnerable and broken, and ultimately, for demonstrating the depth of God's love for humankind. What will we ever achieve if we only look at our own human limitations? If we just focus on doing small things which feel achievable, what will ever be accomplished in this world? What would ever be built, what would be started, and what would ever change?

Building a new hospital in Syria raised an obvious question: was it safe and sensible to undertake such a project at this time? The land bought was in a location which had not been hit by the fighting that had devastated other parts of the city. There was no visible destruction, unlike in other places, where it was so extensive. It was a safe place, and people had sought refuge there.

Some zones around the city had remained under the control of extremist fighters since the early part of the conflict when they first took those areas. But the fighters, their families and their supporters had now been moved out of many of these places, and the city began to have a greater sense of peace. Certain areas were still under a greater degree of military control, but the area surrounding the land we had bought was safe and untouched. Land in this area was at a premium price. We were blessed with a low purchase price. Eighteen months later we were told the land had more than quadrupled in value.

Dr A had been talking with local architects in the previous weeks. Five days after embracing this vision, he was given a passage in the Bible after praying for God's guidance. He had generally felt that God didn't speak to him in this way, through praying then opening the Bible, but instead spoke directly to him.

Yet a few weeks before, he had prayed and asked God what he wanted to say to him that day, and had then opened the Bible at a random page. It immediately fell open at Zechariah 1 and 2, which were on facing pages in the English Bible I had given him. He read the passage, then took a photo of the pages and sent them to me.

I was doing the school run and was in a hurry when I first saw them, so skimmed through the passage quickly. I didn't catch its significance at the time.

'Did you see the bit about Jerusalem?' I could hear the intrigue in his voice.

'Oh, yes, I did notice.' I hadn't really made a connection. The signal was poor and we kept having to repeat ourselves.

Over the next couple of days, he asked me again about the

passage, but then left it, as he must have sensed my lack of response.

One sunny morning five days after finding this new, big vision for the hospital, I decided I wanted to dedicate some time to praying. I had parked close to the beach so that I could sit on the pebbles, breathing in the sea air and enjoying God's beautiful creation while I spent time praying.

I had received a message earlier in the morning from a woman whom I hadn't been in touch with for at least eighteen months. It came out of the blue, and in it she said she had had a dream about me in which I was looking for a lot of money for a project but didn't have enough. In the dream, there was a man who was able to provide it. I wondered if the dream was linked to our hospital ...

A message came through from Dr A.

'Samara, you won't believe this.'

'What happened? Tell me!'

His next message was a photo of his Bible again, showing the same passage of Zechariah 1 and 2.

'I just asked God what he wanted to show me today. I opened the Bible randomly and it was this same passage again. I thought maybe there was something wrong with the book which makes it keep opening in the same place. I tried opening it a couple more times, but each time it opened at a different passage.'

Intrigued, I called him.

'Remind me what it says,' I probed.

'It is talking about a man taking the measurements for the Temple of Jerusalem. This is what we are doing now with the engineers for Grace (Jerusalem) Hospital.'

'Does it say that? I need to read it again.' I looked up the passage. My eyes scanned Zechariah 1:16:

'Therefore, this is what the LORD says: I have returned to show mercy to Jerusalem. My Temple will be rebuilt, says the LORD of Heaven's Armies, and measurements will be taken for the reconstruction of Jerusalem.' (NLT)

This was so close to our hearts, as when I received the passage to evacuate our first field hospital, it was talking about the Temple and Jerusalem being attacked and destroyed. As I read on to chapter 2, I reread verses 1–5 a few times:

> When I looked again, I saw a man with a measuring line in his hand. 'Where are you going?' I asked. He replied, 'I am going to measure Jerusalem, to see how wide and how long it is.' Then the angel who was with me went to meet a second angel who was coming toward him. The other angel said, 'Hurry, and say to that young man, "Jerusalem will someday be so full of people and livestock that there won't be room enough for everyone! Many will live outside the city walls. Then I, myself, will be a protective wall of fire around Jerusalem, says the LORD. And I will be the glory inside the city!"' (NLT)

This passage also seemed so significant as there were so many similarities between what took place in Jerusalem when the Babylonians invaded and what had happened in the city where we planned to build the hospital. Jerusalem lost most of its people, and many people had also fled from parts of this Syrian city. The events which took place in parts of this city were similar to some of the violent events the Babylonians inflicted on Jerusalem and the Israelites when they besieged Jerusalem. When the king of the Israelites escaped one night, he was captured and forced to watch as his sons were killed in front of him. In the same way, many people who had not escaped in time from these areas of this city that fell under siege had had to watch as members of their families were beheaded.

Parts of this city had been besieged, as Jerusalem had been. When districts had been taken, some of the residents had fled, some were killed, some were beheaded and some were kidnapped and ransomed, and the fighters and their families moved into the homes of the people they had killed and forced out. Other people were taken as prisoners, just as the Israelites had been taken away as exiles, and some of the poorest left behind to work the land.

Parts of this city were fairly deserted once these armed groups had been forced back out, but the destruction left behind in these parts was mind-blowing. However, areas the fighters had left slowly started to become repopulated, as some who had fled took the opportunity to return.

I had visited someone in this city who was helping with our work. He showed me his neighbourhood which had been under siege. He had witnessed terrifying violence and destruction, the streets surrounding his apartment becoming deserted and very badly damaged. He and his wife were the only people left in their apartment block. He had pointed out to me the objects they had hidden behind, when they had been trying to get out of their home and across the street, to escape being shot.

It was difficult to gain accurate figures in a changing environment where information was often regarded as classified intelligence. Estimates suggested that nearly two million people were living in this governorate, yet there wasn't an adequately resourced, fully functioning hospital in it that could provide free medical care which included specialist services for intermediate to advanced cases.

Chapter 2 of Zechariah felt like an assurance that in the future this area, and this hospital, would be completely filled again, with a 'protective wall of fire' around it, and with God's Holy Spirit being 'the glory inside the city'.

A couple of weeks later, after praying, we were led to Zechariah 4 in the same way. We felt that verses 6–7 were God's promises to us as they were to Zerubbabel who rebuilt the Temple:

> This is what the LORD says to Zerubbabel: it is not by force nor by strength, but by my Spirit, says the LORD of Heaven's Armies. Nothing, not even a mighty mountain, will stand in Zerubbabel's way; it will become a level plain before him! And when Zerubbabel sets the final stone of the Temple in place, the people will shout: 'May God bless it! May God bless it!' (NLT)

We felt so encouraged, and verse 10 also had special meaning for us:

Do not despise these small beginnings, for the LORD rejoices to see the work begin, to see the plumb line in Zerubbabel's hand. (NLT)

This was especially relevant as we had that same day been discussing the height of the building and whether there would be floors underground. I had looked up the meaning of a plumb line and was fascinated to learn that it is a tool to gauge height and depth, as well as ensuring the vertical line or straightness of a building.

Often God asks us to do his work in a counter-cultural way. He asks us to do things which, from a human perspective, seem risky or unwise. But I believe God wants us to aim high for his work. Jesus told us if we had faith the size of a mustard seed, we could move mountains. Why do we have trouble believing this? Why should we doubt that something amazing could happen in our lives, rather than just reading or hearing about it in a book or in someone else's life? Why do people confine miracles to simply being historical events that took place in the Bible? God has not changed since the Bible was written. What makes someone else more useable to God than me or you? We should not be afraid to have a big vision for God's kingdom, to dream big dreams for serving some of the most basic needs of the poorest in our world, just because it seems too big, or even impossible, with our limited abilities. We should remember that throughout history God has used the most unexpected people to accomplish the most amazing things.

How many miracles that have happened in this world would never have taken place if someone had been too scared to ask for them? Every miracle started with a problem. Every sign and wonder in the Bible took place when someone had no choice but to depend on God. We should see these challenging places we arrive at in life not as problems or disasters but as opportunities. We should all be praying for more of these events, and for the vision to see them not as problems to be solved with limited human logic, but as opportunities for God to be glorified. We need to listen very carefully to that 'still, small voice of calm', so easily ignored, as I believe worldly strategy and rationale, although they have their place, can also be some of the biggest killers of miracles, and of living the faith Jesus asked us to have – the faith to move mountains.

Faith is not something we simply receive or possess and keep in our hearts. We have to 'step out of the boat' in order for our faith to be realised and lived. It is like a recipe. If you start off making something at God's calling, and then add a problem which cannot be solved easily, applying prayer and active faith, or dependence on God, for a solution, then the result is something bigger and more amazing than we could have cooked up ourselves.

I also believe God meets us in the place where we are doing something for all the right reasons, not out of selfish ambition or because we will get something in return, but out of a simple desire to demonstrate his love and see his name and his kingdom lifted up. When we are serving the poorest, the most vulnerable, without any benefit for ourselves, this is when I feel he is most active. But I also believe that loving and serving others is the most beneficial and rewarding experience any of us could ever hope to have in life, so we cannot fail to benefit and will gain much in return.

Jesus promised that when we make his kingdom our priority, God will supply everything we need (Matt. 6:33). This is my understanding of why we have seen so many amazing results and events in our work. This is the reason I have certainty we can trust him to provide everything needed, right down to the last stone, and the last piece of equipment.

13

The Children of Aleppo

November 2017

Six months after my first trip, I returned to Aleppo. The change in the atmosphere, as well as in our team's morale, was obvious. Back in April, just four months after the siege of east Aleppo had been broken, I had felt the weight of the pain they were carrying, as well as the suffering and trauma they had been through. It was visible in their posture and imprinted on their faces. The sounds of explosions and gunfire had still been part of daily life, even if more distant than before.

But when I went back in November, their faces looked relaxed and I saw them smiling real smiles of relief and hope. I asked one of our team how the situation was in Aleppo now. I was surprised by his reply: 'Good! It is really great now!' he said. In comparison with how it had been over the preceding years, this was certainly true. I didn't hear any guns or explosions during this visit. The security situation had vastly improved. This was life-changing, but the poverty levels were still excruciating for many. I saw children scavenging in bins, something the people there said would not have happened in Aleppo before the war.

On this trip I saw with my own eyes the toll this brutal war has taken on the children of Syria, and the heavy burdens they had now been forced to carry. On one day I encountered four children in Aleppo who all made an impression on me, contrasting starkly and heartbreakingly with our own children back in the UK. Only one of these four children was linked with our aid work; the three others we simply met during the very limited time we spent getting food.

One beautiful boy was alone on the streets of Aleppo selling biscuits. Adorable and endearing, yet persistent and focused, this boy couldn't have been more than nine years old. Yet he was already an experienced professional who had learnt how to make his quota for the day. We didn't know who he was working for – perhaps his parents, or someone else using him to make a profit for themselves.

As we queued at the falafel store, another boy, thin and dressed in dirty old clothing, told us he was hungry. He said he was from a displaced family, and the strain of life was evident on his young face. We bought him lunch and invited him to come to one of the distribution centres to get some warmer clothes as he looked freezing standing there in a thin top and grubby old trousers. It was cold in the rain in Aleppo at this time of year, and on those days I couldn't feel any great difference from the weather we had had in the UK before my trip.

Later, we went to distribute clothes and hygiene items to forty-one displaced families housed in an old sports institute. They were living in extremely poor conditions, with decaying walls and no glass in the windows. The residents showed us a boy who was very shy. When we had visited the settlement during daylight hours he had been at work, but by the time we returned in the evening with clothes and shoes, he had returned. His father had been killed a few years before and his mother had no way of supporting the family.

He held out his hands to show me the evidence of the hard labour he has no choice but to take on. This twelve-year-old boy does not go to school like our children, but instead goes to work every day in a plastic recycling and production plant. He works from 9.00 a.m. to 7.00 p.m. every day just to survive and support his mother and siblings. As a result, he does not have anything close to an acceptable standard of living. His mother and siblings have returned to their original home, but there is no opportunity to earn an income there, so this poor boy lives with his aunt and her three children in one room, and is now the breadwinner for all of them as well. Wow.

This little boy and his story truly broke my heart. He is no longer a boy, but is instead a man, years ahead of his time. He is not just any man though. He is a noble gentleman living with

a true sense of honour and commitment, and he already understands his responsibility in life. This innocent child is paying the
price for the stupidity and greed of adults who should have (but
haven't) learnt the simple lessons this boy has already had to
learn in his short life. But he is not alone.

There are so many other little ones who should have enough
food and clothes, and who should have an education, but instead
they have been robbed of all of these. I was deeply moved and
humbled by that boy's shy but beautiful eyes and smile. He is a
living example of sacrifice, and I keep asking myself what he
could teach our children, who live in a parallel universe which
exists in the same world we share with him, about honour, duty
and life.

In the evening we had my favourite Middle Eastern dish for
dinner: *molokhia*. My step-grandfather, a Lebanese-Egyptian,
used to make it for us, and it is now a celebrated and sought-
after family classic. It draws members of my family from across
the UK to come and share it if one of us announces we are
making it. We sat outside to eat in the cold. I was recovering
from a cough that would have been exacerbated by the smoky
interior of the sheesha bar. I felt a little frustrated as we had
ordered far too much food for our group. As we sat commenting
on the amount of food left over, a grubby little girl appeared
by our table.

Just like the boy we had met earlier, she was selling biscuits.
And like the boy, she had a disarming confidence and determination which came from having spent her early years fending
for herself in an unprotected and dangerous environment. For
her, there was no room for the luxury of complacency or of
living for pleasure. This girl has learnt already that life is about
survival.

I was shocked to find out that she was just eight years old,
the same age as my eldest child. I shuddered to think about the
dangers a girl of this age, alone in the streets on a dark night
in the city, might face. It was unsettling to see it from this
perspective, as a mother with a little child the same age. My
children didn't even walk alone to the end of our street in a

very safe and protected area in broad daylight. There were so many stark contrasts between my children and these, separated not just by distance, but by injustice, imbalance and a completely different existence.

The girl asked us about the leftovers still sitting on our table, and my frustration at the excess immediately gave way to relief that we had ordered way too much. I wished we had even more to give her, as no doubt there would be many hungry tummies in her family in need of something nutritious.

As we sat munching the biscuits we had bought from her, I couldn't help but reflect on the huge amount of need I had seen in such a short space of time. In the places we visit we expect to find people with great needs, and we certainly do find them. But the stark reality of the life stories we are told never fails to exceed what I expected to hear and see or to increase my understanding of the harsh and tough existence of living a disadvantaged life in a place like Syria.

But three of the four children I encountered that day were not in the places we set out to visit, we simply came across them during the very short time we were out on the streets of Aleppo.

They are just some of the children who motivate and inspire our orphans and widows project, which has been one of the hardest and most complicated projects to implement in Syria. Reaching out to children and families like these in such a socially, economically and culturally complex war environment is a difficult task if we want to achieve something more meaningful than just a simple aid handout. The needs go so much deeper than merely filling the stomachs of these people.

I feel strongly that, as adults and as humanity living comfortable lives in the West, we should be learning from these children. Having seen the persistence of these young biscuit sellers and their fight for survival, we should learn some of their qualities of focus, determination and pushiness, and we should employ these qualities to fight for the rights and needs of children like these, to be a voice for the voiceless, to bring relief to those who are poor, and hope to those who are hopeless.

Our challenge lies in being disadvantaged by the many distractions in our culture of pleasure-seeking and complacency. It is harder to think in great depth about such things when we live such comfortable lives. But I ask myself a question. At the end of my life, when I am called to account for my actions and omissions (because I believe we will all have to do this), how will I justify the comfortable life I have lived in the UK while this injustice exists around us in our global community? When I breathe my last breath, what will my answer be to the question 'are you satisfied with what you achieved in your life, and with how you used the things you were given for the benefit of the people around you who didn't have the same opportunities and resources as you did?'

At the moment my answer to this question is no. I am not satisfied. I haven't done enough. I could give more. I could make more sacrifices in my life to help someone less fortunate.

This is exactly what Jesus was talking about when he said to a rich young man that he should sell his possessions and give them to the poor. If we have possessions, and someone else can't afford to eat, we still have something to give. Most of us in the West are rich in comparison with those who are poor in Syria, or in other Third World countries.

It is not just me who has felt God's direct call to this work, as a number of other people who have got involved with our appeal have told me fascinating accounts of how they first came to get in touch with me.

During the second appeal I did at the end of 2014, a woman made contact after hearing me give an interview on one of the Christian radio stations. She told me later that it was strange how she ended up hearing the interview as she had been alone in the house cleaning and had put the radio on to listen to some music while she worked. There were a number of pre-set channels, of which the Christian radio station was one. She was nowhere near the radio but told me it had changed from one channel to the other on its own. She thought it odd, but started to listen, wondering whether there was something God wanted her to hear. After listening to my appeal for people to help collect clothing, she immediately got in contact and started to organise a collection for us.

Around the same time another woman got in contact. She had a dream of a woman packing up aid to send out to the displaced people in the Middle East, and then she woke in the middle of the night. She wasn't sure whether the woman in the dream was herself or someone else, but felt unsettled by it and couldn't get back to sleep. She started searching the internet and found the details of my appeal, but continued searching and then found the details of the company that does our shipping and that specialises in transporting aid. The next day she got in touch with them, explaining that she felt called to do something to help. They told her to contact me. She immediately got involved and has been one of our most faithful collectors, as well as running a storage hub for us. She is one of our great prayer team.

Around a year later another woman got in contact, explaining how I had done a work placement with her community rehabilitation team while I was a nursing student around ten years before. I hadn't seen or heard from anyone there since I left the placement, even through social media. She said she had become a Christian since I had left and had moved to a different area. One day she had been hoovering when my name randomly came to her mind. She found it strange as she had had no reason to think about me in years, but she remembered I had been a Christian and started to search my name on the internet. She was amazed to see the appeal I was doing, and when we spoke she was convinced God wanted her to get involved, so she began organising an appeal at her church.

God gives us small nudges to do things to make a big difference. These little stories, followed by the faithfulness and obedience of these people to get involved, provide encouragement that we are on the right path. Sometimes I wonder how different my life might have looked if I hadn't been willing to respond to my 'nudges' or calling. I can't bear to imagine the things that might not have been! These little nudges are some of the many ways God communicates with us; they are so easily ignored or dismissed in a culture which is largely out of touch with events which cannot be scientifically explained, and which might instead be explained as coincidences. Yet, I believe God really wants us to pay close attention when he does choose to use prompts like these. He is an interactive God, bigger than our understanding of life and the universe, and we should be ready to hear and respond if he chooses an unusual way to get our attention.

We all have something we can give, and each of us has something special to offer, whether we realise it or not. Just as the body is made up of many different parts which all work together to make a person function, an appeal like this is also made up of many different people, skills, attributes, resources and availability of time – and all of these are needed for us to function.

It was always my vision not to let our work become about raising money to finance and fuel a machine here in the UK. It is important to me that the money we raise is spent as much as possible on providing the support needed elsewhere. The warehouses we have used in the UK have been kindly donated to us. It would be such a shame to commit to spending money on something like this if there are other charities, businesses and even farmers who have spaces we can use for free. Many are willing to give the use of their space as their gift at certain times of the year around our appeal dates. We all have something to offer, and it is my vision to bring together the different resources each person has to enable each one of us to do or give something useful to support our fellow humans in need.

I never wanted to set up a charity. I resisted it for as long as I could, working instead under the umbrella of another charity. But there came a point when I had to accept that we had grown too much for it to be fair to continue to ask this other charity to deal with the governance of our work, or for us to be independently working under another charity's umbrella. They continue to be a fantastic partner of ours, however, and a great blessing.

Paying for our shipping costs was a necessary overhead for us from the beginning. It was unavoidable as we needed our aid to be moved on specific days and times and, ultimately, moving containers across oceans costs money. We also needed to rely on a professional service rather than depending on goodwill in this instance. Where our work in Syria is concerned, I began to see that we also had a duty to look after the people who help us distribute the huge volumes of aid we were sending. It was too much work to give to volunteers, as they also need money to afford to eat. Income levels are now generally very low in Syria, and the majority of people struggle to make ends meet. At the time of writing, 85% of the population is living in poverty. Providing even just a little money to someone who is helping us, restores some dignity in their life, and it is right to provide some level of paid employment in that depleted economy. It also helps us establish clear distinctions for our workers between those who receive our aid and those who distribute it, many of whom might not be much better off than the people we are helping.

We have not spent money on marketing, advertising or postal campaigns, to date. Even our volunteers who help with our accounts and with writing thank-you letters give what they can, buying stamps from their own pocket for those we can't thank by email. Occasionally, one of our supporters will send in a sheet of stamps to help with this, for which we are grateful. These are the little details which make the difference between a charity with significant overheads and a charity which tries to avoid every possible overhead.

Sometimes, doing it this way makes my mission much harder as I have to wait longer for a volunteer to help with our admin or graphic design, or for a storage space to be offered by someone willing to donate some space rent-free. Doing it this way means we haven't relied on paid fundraisers or on any other means of generating income, we simply have to rely on people taking responsibility for their part in this process, whether that's helping raise the money needed to send the boxes of clothes they have collected, providing a storage space we can use at the end of each appeal to load our containers, or helping with our IT, PR or admin – all of it is needed.

Our very small core team and our lack of paid or full-time staff in the UK mean we don't always manage to thank donors or change our website as quickly as we would like. But I also know many of our supporters are happy to support us because they know where their money is going.

We simply have to keep talking to people, keep asking, keep praying and keep waiting for God to provide. But this makes the journey more exciting, too, as the things we needed most have had a mysterious way of turning up after we have prayed in faith and waited expectantly on God.

14

A Widowed Christian and a Soldier in Homs

November 2017

It was the nicest of all the homes of displaced widows I had visited. There was a sofa to sit on, for one thing, and even a picture hanging over peeling paint on an otherwise bare wall – a depiction of Jesus, the hallmark of most traditional Syrian Christian families' homes. As the crown of thorns drew blood from his forehead, his pain-filled eyes looked directly at this middle-aged woman, whose eyes, in turn, were cast down at the little cup of *ahway*, the traditional Syrian coffee, on her knee. Having suffered a death similar to those inflicted by the jihadist groups in Syria, he truly understands suffering, I thought. The widow sipped silently at her strong black coffee.

Through her grief-ridden face she strained a smile before pouring out her heart. Her original home had been in a Christian area in Homs. Her family had been well off. She and her husband were educated, had jobs and owned their own house and land, and their children had been studying at university.

The al-Nusra fighters had come with guns during the night while they were sleeping. The militants forced their way into their home and dragged the woman's husband roughly from their bed. He was just an ordinary man, not a politician, not a fighter. His only 'crime' was being a Christian. They were coming back, they had said, and if she was still there when they returned, they would take her too.

Terror-stricken, she fled in her nightdress in the dead of night, trying to comprehend the nightmare she had found herself in. Similar events had been desecrating lives and families across Syria. People could scarcely believe what they were seeing and hearing about, gruesome acts and barbarism, shattering their communities and their nation. Yet none ever believed it could happen in their district. But now it was happening to them. Now it was their home, their family, their neighbourhood. Now it was her husband.

When her slippers came off in the mud as she ran, she kept running, not daring to stop to pick them up. She ran and ran, not knowing where to go or when it might be safe for her to stop to catch her breath. Her home, her refuge, the place she had raised her children, her community had been violated. Where could she go now to find any sense of safety or security?

Shortly afterwards, the armed group offered her husband's release for a ransom. She emptied their bank accounts and begged and borrowed money to collect the fortune that had been demanded. They released him after she paid. But he was a different man. He had been beaten and tortured. He was shattered. He had escaped from one nightmare to find he now faced a new kind. With no home to go back to, they had lost everything they had ever had and worked for, including their savings. How could they start over or begin to pick up the pieces of their broken lives? They became one of the statistics, the internally displaced, of whom there were around six and a half million at the time. They were one of the hordes of families who had lost everything. After a couple of weeks, his heart could take no more of the torment of this broken world. This newly destitute, displaced man died of a heart attack.

An unmarried Christian woman I had visited earlier that morning had been from the same area. She had been elsewhere in the city when, three years before, al-Nusra came. As she was driving home her brother called. His panic-stricken voice begged her not to return. The fighters were killing their neighbours in the street. Her only option was to turn back. Her eyes filled with tears as she told me that was the last time she heard her brother's voice. She, too, lives in rented accommodation now, unfurnished and paid for by other members of her community. I felt her shoulders shudder as I held her, telling her there are many of us praying for them.

Three years after these events, al-Nusra and the people connected with them were still living in the homes of those they had killed and forced out. The widow was one of the lucky ones as most of her family had survived. Others had simply been murdered in their beds or in the street. Anyone unsupportive of the ideology of an Islamist group, and of the creation of an Islamic government ruled by harsh Sharia law, was either killed, kidnapped and ransomed, or taken as a prisoner or slave. Some people disappeared and were never heard from again. In many of the areas that were under seige, those who did not escape in time were restricted from leaving, as their presence in this area made it difficult for the army to retaliate, or to return homes, buildings and land to their original owners – namely, the people who had worked and earned the money to buy and build these houses. If these armed groups could keep innocent civilians in this area with them, it bought them valuable time and protection through the cheapest and most effective defence system possible. Who would attack them while they had innocent women, children and elderly people interwoven among them?

As we talked with the widow, a young man in his late twenties walked confidently into the room. He was her son. He had been conscripted for his compulsory military service just before the start of the conflict. After completing the mandatory two years of service expected of all Syrian men, he had to forget any hope of discharge as the country was by then at war. Every eligible man aged between eighteen and forty-two was needed, and on many occasions, men were taken from the street or from their workplaces to serve. Although there were a few exemptions, such as being a priest or religious leader, an only son, or in full-time study, men of a certain age came to avoid travelling through certain areas and checkpoints through fear of being conscripted. Once enlisted, very few were discharged in the height of the conflict. Many had no choice but to quietly accept their fate, and pray.

Many of those who met the criteria for conscription fled the country, some via people smugglers using dangerous routes, risking their lives and the lives of their families. The men who lived in areas held by other fighting groups also often tried to keep themselves hidden as the militant and jihadist groups were even less discriminating about who they forced to fight alongside them. I heard an account from an elderly grandmother living in Latakia who had been imprisoned in Idlib, and who described how her grandson had been taken at the age of twelve, radicalised, and forced to fight.

There was no true salary for these soldiers in the Syrian army. Even many of the officers, who were paid more than the ordinary soldiers, did not generally get much more than one hundred dollars per month. They could not easily feed a family, even for a week, when other necessary living expenses were taken into account. Doctors, lawyers, engineers and other professionals who were conscripted found themselves being forced from their homes with their families when they could no longer pay for them, unless they had savings to live off, or could somehow find another salary alongside their army service, and this was a struggle. Many families had faced the anguish of being driven into poverty in this way. Husbands and fathers were no longer able to be breadwinners but instead became a financial burden to the family as the food and living costs alone would amount to more than they were compensated for when giving their lives and their blood to serve their country. Many of these men would not see their families for long periods if posted in a different area as they would not be able to find the money to travel back to see them in their time off unless their family could help them with the costs.

These men and their families were completely torn. On the one hand, few volunteered to join the army, but on the other hand, who else would there be to take back their homes and neighbourhoods from the multitude of jihadist groups that were taking over large parts of the country? Who else would there be to enable any kind of hope for a normal existence for the next generation of Syrians? Who else would there be to protect their mothers, grandparents and children from the multitude of deadly Islamist armies that had torn the country apart and moved across their homeland committing unspeakable crimes against humanity? They felt it was their duty to protect their families and their country, and there was no way to escape it. If they didn't, no one else would do it.

This young man had now served eight years in the army. This long and traumatic time was hardened onto his face. There was a distance in his eyes. His taut, muscular body showed a fit young man at the prime of his life. Yet the way he carried himself and moved showed a poise and alertness that he had been forced to develop merely to survive during this harrowing experience.

His mother's weary eyes followed him tenderly as he moved across the room and sat with us to say hello for a few moments. As I watched his toughened figure swagger in and pull up a chair before sitting down, my heart melted as I looked at him through the eyes of a mother. I thought of the legions of young men like this one, on each side, whose lives had been stolen by such an evil war. His mother would have watched, day by day, the way her precious boy metamorphosed from an innocent child into a determined and cynical soldier. How many lives had her boy had to take in his own short life? I was sure the aspirations she had dared to dream for him as he was growing up made a harsh contrast with the life he now led. The unprovoked, ruthless cruelty his mother and father had suffered along with the rest of their community when al-Nusra took their neighbourhood would likely have deepened the all-consuming rage in this young man's broken heart, as well as his resolve to put a stop to the fighters who had robbed them of their dignity and stolen their futures and their dreams.

Even if the conflict ended that day and he found himself free to decide how to live his future, what kind of life could a man like this hope for after everything his eyes had seen, and after all the things he had had to do? His youth had been stolen from him, along with his hopes and ambitions, and for the last eight years his heart and soul had been little more than captives in his young body. When he left, his mother told us she prayed every day for him. She did not pray he would come home, for she had seen other sons brought home to their mothers, but they were brought home dead. Her prayer was humble: it was simply that he would live.

As we sat talking I wondered, as a mother of young boys, what had been hardest for her – losing her home and her husband, or watching her beloved son being transformed gradually over these years into a toughened soldier. Did they talk about his obligations in the army? Probably not. For many people in this horrific situation, it was undoubtedly better to leave the obvious unspoken.

We drove away through the wreckage of Hamadiyah, where collapsed concrete floors of tower blocks lay like fallen sets of vertically stacked dominoes. I talked with Haitham about the widow's son. That young man and his reality had really moved my heart. Haitham told me of his relative who was in a similar situation. His relative had confessed to him feeling that even if he were discharged, he wouldn't have anything to offer a woman in marriage after eight years of military service – no job, no income, no home, no future. No doubt he would bring with him a huge amount of emotional trauma and psychological challenge. I have heard stories of parents refusing to allow the marriage of their daughters to men who are in the army or who are likely to be called up. Who can blame them? The injustice of a meaningless war permeates every layer of society. No one escapes it.

The hardest thing for me was to leave knowing that there was little we could do for this widow other than pray, and give her a dignity bag filled with women's hygiene items and new underwear. Her other children had fled abroad and, for many families, relatives who have left Syria are as good as gone for now. Most will not see their relatives again until the war is over, whenever that may be. Many of those who have left may still fear returning after this; some fear conscription, and others fear being questioned over their reasons for leaving and about their connections outside the country. Trust is at rock bottom for everyone, on every side.

This widow's haunting story is something I will never forget, but there are many widows in Syria with similar stories whose living circumstances are worse. As a small organisation, our resources are directed to those in the most hopeless of situations – the widows with young children who would struggle to work even if they could find a job, the widows trying to survive in unfinished buildings, tents or abandoned schools. There are too many, and their needs are ... *overwhelming*.

Over time we have seen that simply giving the basic essentials for living to widows and those taking care of orphans is not always the best way to help. We have begun to focus more on building up and encouraging these women to be independent. Providing a woman with the training or resources she needs to establish an income of her own builds her sense of self-worth, as well as a future to work towards, rather than creating a feeling of dependency and need. Whether providing courses for women to gain new skills, or sewing machines and fabric, or even connections and moral support to help them find jobs, these are the things which help rebuild lives.

If people feel moved by a story we share, God calls to their heart for them to respond as individuals. Many do respond, and my heart, for one, is willing to help everyone we can. Each of us should be willing to give our individual portion to make it possible to help. How many of the poorest of the poor have gone without in this world because someone was moved by compassion in seeing their situation and hearing their story, but then continued with their life as normal, expecting someone else to provide? Who else will provide?

It is up to us. Can we pray, asking God to provide for them, if we are not willing to first give what we have available to us? Whether what we have is little or large, we should be willing to give it. If we are willing to give what we have in our hands, what we can afford or even what we can't, then how much more will God multiply our heartfelt gifts given in love and mercy? The feeding of the five thousand took place after the only available food had been put forward – two fish and five loaves of bread. It was nowhere near enough. It was a laughable amount to contribute to the feeding of a group of this size, but once it was given willingly, God multiplied it so that it was enough to feed infinitely more people than science would have said was possible.

15

Hope in the Rubble of Deir ez-Zor

May 2018

After I arrived back in Syria in May 2018, my second night was spent in Damascus under rocket attack. It was a shocking and terrifying experience on every level. Clearly we weren't expecting the attack, otherwise I would not have stayed there that night. We left the next morning for a safer area. For the next few days, my nerves were on edge and I found myself jumping at every noise, even in the distance. So many of those noises seemed to bear some kind of resemblance to the sound of an explosion. This baptism by fire set the scene for what was a very intense couple of weeks in Syria.

There are some places in the world in which you simply can't imagine any human could live. The area around Ar Rahmie Hospital in Deir ez-Zor was one of them. As the scrapes of my footsteps echoed through the empty, rubble-filled street, I was stunned to hear a woman singing from upstairs in one of the damaged buildings. I could hardly believe a family was living in this chaos. Not a single house was intact, and rubble was heaped up on either side of the road, blocking the entrances of most of the homes. Yet this family was not alone. Nor was this a unique street. As we walked and drove around this and the surrounding area, I could see that every road in this district of the city was as damaged and destroyed as this one.

The road to Deir ez-Zor tells its own tale of conflict and unrest. As we moved out of Homs, the major checkpoint going towards Palmyra was more demanding than the others, requiring a list of the names of all passengers in each vehicle as well as details of where they were travelling to and from. Soon we stopped en route at a small shop housing a café filled with men wearing military uniforms, and with rifles slung over their shoulders. As we moved on, one young injured soldier stood at a checkpoint, his arm in a sling, watching the cars passing through.

The abandoned city of Palmyra appeared on the road. Before the war it was home to more than 50,000 people and was frequented by many visitors and workers from outside. It had been taken twice by ISIS, and twice taken back again by the Syrian army, and as a result the former residents had not yet returned to this uncertain city – it now stood silent, little more than a ghost city of empty buildings that had lost their hearts.

This was no longer a civilian area, and the only place to buy fuel at Palmyra now was a one-pump petrol station. A man in army uniform filled up the tanks as I surveyed the surroundings. The remnants suggested that it had previously been a bigger, thriving petrol station. The walls were now peppered with cavities left by bullets pelted at the walls, as well as with gaping holes exposed by heavier artillery. I couldn't help but try to imagine the scenes this place had been host to, and which had left such a sight behind.

Who were the men who had fought here? What was their part in this conflict, and what occupied their hearts and minds as they hid behind these walls with bullets piercing anything in their path? What did their fear feel like? How many men's lives were sacrificed here, leaving grieving relatives to pick up the pieces of family left behind?

So little along the isolated desert road gave the impression of anything inhabited, or habitable. It was hard to believe we would find another city if we kept driving. The landscape was broken up by the occasional ruins of buildings that had seen happier days. Carcasses of burnt-out vehicles martyred in the line of duty lay scattered by the roadside.

A couple of mini tornadoes sucked up columns of sand beside the long and deserted road which became more and more empty the further east we drove. The damaged bridges and roads were pointed out to me, some destroyed by foreign air strikes that left craters in the tarmac which had since filled with sand. They still proved to be a hazard, and it was not long before our team in the car in front was forced to stop to change a tyre, blown out by a hole in the road.

One thing I didn't anticipate was rain in the desert. Syria had experienced uncharacteristic and torrential rain in a number of cities over the preceding weeks. This explained some of the random pools of water by the roadside – even streams in a few places. These must have been the water source for the occasional isolated patches of greenery found in the desert sand.

One last major checkpoint signalled our arrival at the forgotten city of Deir ez-Zor, resting on the historic and biblically signif-icant Euphrates River. It was an emotional sight to see so many broken and abandoned buildings. Each of these places had housed the desires and visions of generations, but now lay destroyed. Birthing dreams and making them a reality takes time, commit-ment and perseverance, often over many years. Destroying them, however, can take seconds. The city was filled with dreams cast aside and hopes postponed. But that was why we were there.

'Do you recognise anything?' Haitham asked, smiling, as we turned from a bomb-ravaged street to park in the shade of a less damaged building. Surely our hospital could not be in the middle of all these ruins, I thought, as I peered through the windscreen. I was greeted by the familiar sight of a forty-foot container, painted white, which we had originally sent filled with aid from the UK. It had been converted, and we had been using it as an operating department at Ar Rahmie Hospital since it had opened three months earlier.

As the streets and buildings around our little field hospital were all so terribly damaged and destroyed, I was surprised to see an informal shop stall open for business in the rubble at the foot of a building's carcass. This, along with long bunches of drying garlic and lines of washing hung out from the gaps where windows would once have been, was evidence that people were still living in these ruins.

The charred chassis of a bus lay on the street opposite Ar Rahmie, and the adjacent apartment blocks were smothered with deep pockmarks inflicted while the conflict was at its worst.

It had hit hard in this area of Jabaeli in Deir ez-Zor. I found myself wondering who was inside those residential buildings while they were being shot at, and who was firing the weapons. Some walls were smeared with black patches of soot left in the wake of fires, most likely started by weapons. I had known our hospital was serving an area in desperate need, and had seen pictures of the better side of the road, but I had not imagined the extent of the damage in the area directly surrounding the hospital itself.

Even the building functioning as our small hospital had a mended blast hole in the side. The room now used as our laboratory had been patched up with breeze blocks and cement, and the rest of the exterior walls were peppered with the scars left behind by bullets. The building on the other side of the road had many front walls missing on each floor, and some of the concrete floors now sagged. Yet people lived there.

When I surveyed the tremendous destruction and the scale of the damage, which was more extensive than anyone outside Syria could imagine, I could hardly comprehend the amount of time, money and energy that has been channelled into creating these post-apocalyptic scenes. Are humans really capable of this?

Deir ez-Zor had been on my heart for about a year. It had caught my attention as there was so much fighting there, yet it was rarely mentioned in our media. Dr A had told me what a poor and simple area it was, even before the war, and we had discussed using our meditainers there. This was a place where they could provide a service which would be life-saving. Sometimes called the Forgotten City, this place really tugged at my heart.

The city's inhabitants had had five years of violence and fear, the first two from al-Nusra and the last three from ISIS, which kept it under a brutal and oppressive control. The fighting to free this area was ruthless, too. Now everyone was tentatively breathing a sigh of relief, and our aid had been distributed to more than 80,000 people in December 2017 after ISIS was forced out. Yet the regularity with which gunfire rang out in the after-noons and evenings maintained a level of unease, serving as a reminder that the war here was not yet over. Fighting still persisted in other parts of the governorate, and tensions still remained on the oil-rich eastern side of the Euphrates River too.

Our team had been seeing around 3,000 of these poor people each month at Ar Rahmie, in the ruins of Deir ez-Zor. We were providing medical care in one of the most damaged areas, and the space we were using wasn't adequate. We needed more spacious operating rooms to enable a wider spectrum of procedures to be carried out, and the women of this area required obstetric care. There were no cardiology services in the governorate, and additional provision was needed for the children too.

The dramatic destruction is unimaginable in both its nature and its extent, yet the greatest damage in Syria is not always as visible. The devastation to humanity, life, community and trust is more significant than the desecration of the buildings and infrastructure. In many cases the harm done to the people is clearly visible: the loss of an arm or leg, a crater left in someone's back and covered in scar tissue, or the multitude of other injuries caused by the array of merciless killing machines. Others nurse wounds of a different nature which cannot be seen so easily; the clues are found in the dull resignation in their weary eyes, in their furrowed brows and in the absence of any expression resembling a smile. But there is yet another kind of damage that isn't given much attention either. It is less sensational than the war injuries and bloody traumas, yet the effects are just as devastating.

Poverty, hand in hand with a medical infrastructure on its knees, has caused an incalculable level of disease and death. It is impossible to compare it with, or add it to, the death and injury toll from the bombs and fighting itself. Many are now dying from conditions which, before the war, were treated effortlessly, and many free of charge. And many now suffer from illnesses only seen in the poorest parts of the world. Many of these poverty-related diseases were not seen in Syria before the war, and those that were seen did not occur on the scale and frequency with which they now occur.

The lack of reliable medical provision, together with the effects of poverty are now among the most significant killers in

Syria. Many of the best, most highly trained doctors left the country to seek a safer future for their families. Nearly two thirds of hospitals across the country either have closed as a result of the loss of doctors, have been damaged or destroyed, or remain open but are largely dysfunctional. No other country in the world comes close to Syria's statistics for attacks on healthcare professionals or facilities, which have become some of the hallmarks of the Syrian conflict.

Poverty has been created during this war on a scale no one in Syria remembers seeing before. It is the quieter killer.

The result was that for the many patients we treated at Ar Rahmie needing more specialist care than our humble little hospital could give, our team didn't have an acceptable hospital to refer them to nearby. Many, when they were asked to go to Damascus or Aleppo, refused as they simply could not make the journey. If they could, they didn't have money to pay for accommodation, or didn't trust that the care they would receive there would be worthy of the significant journey and money needed to stay there and see their treatment through. This is one of the reasons why our vision to build a not-for-profit hospital in Syria is so vitally important.

I had visited a handful of Syrian public hospitals – just about the only hospitals members of the public can walk into and access some kind of free care. Yet, now, many are unable to provide it. If someone gains a diagnosis, there is a high chance they will need to seek treatment privately. Years of conflict, attacks, a depleted economy, sanctions, and a diminished professional workforce have reduced the country's ability to provide an acceptable level of healthcare.

As we visited one public hospital in a different area, we overheard a man talking on the phone. He was frustrated, having brought his son to have a plaster cast taken off his healed broken arm. He said they had been sent away because there was no orthopaedic doctor in the hospital. They couldn't deal with this simple assessment and procedure. It is hard to imagine a hospital of that size or capacity being unable to deal with something so simple.

Our vision is to design and build a hospital which doesn't exist to make a profit, but which, instead, is designed to be an inspirational, forward-thinking hospital, run to a standard which attracts the patients who are able to pay for their care as a way of funding the free and subsidised provision of care for patients who are poor. The land is in an area where a medical school exists, but the main hospitals in which students could train have been destroyed. They are forced to do their practical training in other cities. We want to build a hospital which enables the next generation of doctors to gain the skills, experience and teaching essential to equip them to be able to rebuild their country and serve their people.

Some of the time I spent in Deir ez-Zor on that visit was rather tense. I had been allowed into this area, still under heavy military control, because of my connection with the hospital. But because of the activities of western-linked groups in that area of the country, someone with a British passport would be viewed with a lot of suspicion. During my time at the hospital, we had a number of visits from intelligence officers who asked a lot of questions about me. They were checking we were where we were supposed to be, and wanted to know everything I was doing there. One morning they came and questioned our team there. After much discussion, the team felt uncomfortable taking an English person to visit some of the orphans and widows we had hoped to see.

Later that same day, while we were making that decision, an intelligence officer turned up to question the team about me again. After some time, he left, and the atmosphere shifted. Our coordinator in this area seemed more relaxed, and the team made the decision that we should go to visit one of the orphans and widows before it got dark.

16

Um Ibrahim and Her Fatherless Children

In the Wake of ISIS, May 2018

The gateway, with its double doors, was deceptive: it didn't appear to have been designed for vehicular access. I winced at the screech of metal on metal as the bottom of the chassis ground against the threshold. I had expressed my doubts about the angle of entry, but the driver didn't seem to hold a meagre woman's view in high regard. He didn't appear to hold his car in high esteem either, judging by the glaring crack running from the top to the bottom of his windscreen, with some smaller cracks branching sideways.

But with a few helpful shoves from behind, the car moved forward, kicking up a small cloud of dust from the unmade surface. We pulled into the courtyard of the semi-abandoned school. Sure enough, the car had sustained some new battle scars on its bodywork.

In the area outside the grounds, passionate shouts came from a pitch where a group of young men were playing football. I wondered whether that would have been possible when ISIS had been in control. A crowd of people swarmed around a van parked in the dusty street and giving out hot meals. This, like so many other places, is a deprived area where the majority of people are in dire need.

The sultry evening began to draw in as the sun sank lower in the sky. We approached the school in which Um Ibrahim was living with her children. The gaping windows of the abandoned block, many without glass, looked dim and haunting as we walked towards the bullet-marked building. No longer a busy agent of hope and opportunity, filled with laughter and happy shouts of children playing, it was now simply a dismal skeleton of forgotten dreams.

Flies buzzed around a half-naked baby who rocked himself in a filthy Britax car seat. He strained to reach out for something I couldn't see. My heart sank as I registered the bitter irony that this widow had an old car seat for her baby, but no hope of ever owning a car. A girl of around seven appeared by the baby's side at the sound of our footsteps. Their mother would be back soon, we were told by the girl, who picked up her baby brother, exposing his red, raw bottom.

On cue, a thin figure covered from head to foot in black glided across the courtyard. Only her eyes were visible. I was largely unaccustomed to interacting with women who observe the strictest of Sunni Muslim traditions, and the sight was a little unnerving at first.

Her black-gloved hands reached out to take the baby from her little girl. We followed them in, leaving the men outside. This widow was observing the four months and ten days of mourning required in her community, during which time she should not talk with or be seen by men. She would not leave the home without covering herself in black from head to foot. Some women even cover their eyes.

Immediately after the main entrance, which stood open to all, the corridor was sectioned off by a pair of dirty old curtains hung over a piece of rope. After moving one aside, we found ourselves in the family's squalid living room.

Now, in the presence only of women, she removed the covering from her face before opening the small portion of warm food she had just brought back from the aid van in the street. Her daughter began to devour it. As we sat on the floor, the smell of the one little serving wafted over to us. I doubted that a ration that size would have satisfied me. It could hardly be adequate to feed a hungry family of five. As we sat with the woman on the thin rugs on the floor, her face lacked emotion.

The story of this family had moved me months before when I saw the pictures coming from our aid distributions to more than 80,000 people in Deir ez-Zor in December 2018. This widow was now trying to survive with four children, and no ability to work.

As I sat on the floor with her, I explained that the aid we had given was a gift from some people in the UK who had been praying for her and her family. I told her they were moved by the problems she and her family had experienced and wanted to help. She thanked us and asked God to bless us and our families. I told her my heart was so sad when I heard about what had happened to her husband. She replied humbly that there were many women like her there. I asked where her other children were. She replied that they were out selling bread.

On this particular visit, I was saddened by seeing the numerous bread sellers on the streets, many of whom were children. They weaved in and out of the moving cars, or waited at roundabouts and scoured the rows of traffic, some with clear plastic packs of traditional Arabic flatbreads, and others with bundles of loose rounds hung over their arms in the blazing sun.

After being occupied by ISIS, Deir ez-Zor no longer had a mill for grinding wheat, so this was now being done outside the governorate and the flour was brought in. Needless to say, this pushed up prices in this area which, in the past, had been one of most significant governorates for growing wheat. People in this area now had two options for buying bread: buy it privately and pay a higher price, or buy it from a government bakery for a subsidised rate. For those who take the second option, what they don't spend in money is paid for in time – these bread sellers queue for hours to be able to buy a small portion of bread that some then sell on the streets. Some of the poorest people spend their time queuing in the hope of making a little extra to pay their rent or feed their families. The oldest boy in this family was just thirteen, and was being sent to the streets to sell bread with his younger brother.

I asked the widow what her family needed. She looked at the ground as she replied that they need everything but don't like to ask for anything. I told her that she is my sister. I said to her that her family are my family and mine are hers. If she was in need, she would tell her mother or her sister, and she should do the same with us.

The baby's bottom had been troubling me, so I asked to take a look. He smiled adorably as I looked at his bottom and genitals, which were so red and sore all over. When I asked the mother what had happened, she replied that he was allergic to nappies. Given that he was a baby from such a poor family, it was more likely his skin had reacted to sitting in a sodden nappy of urine and/or faeces for longer periods than the manufacturers had ever intended.

I encouraged the mother to bring the baby to our hospital for treatment, but given her location and the lack of transport, it would be a difficult journey for a woman in mourning, and with three other children, to manage. I took photos of the baby to show one of our doctors later that evening, in order that the cream that he needed could be sent later along with the other things the woman had asked for.

The plight of this family truly challenged me and squeezed my heart in every possible way. If there was one woman I had wanted to be sure to visit in Syria on this trip it was the widowed mother of this dear little baby boy, and the three other children. After I had been sitting with her for a short time we were joined by two neighbours and their children. They asked if we could help them too.

When we left the building, a small group had gathered round the car, including some children and an old man. I watched as one of our team took her own money from her handbag to hand to a dirty, barefoot woman with cropped, uncovered hair and a nervous twitch. The old man told us he was once rich, but now he had nothing.

It was dark as we returned to our hospital, and the security as we came back into the city centre had been tightened. On entering our hospital, we were greeted by one of the cleaners. She followed us up to the office and spoke with our finance manager in Arabic before leaving, looking less hopeful than she had done at the start. I asked him to translate what she had said. She had asked whether we could help her family. She had ten children and was very poor. The needs in that place were over-whelming, and were everywhere we looked. There are some people in Syria who are in the worst of the worst situations, and who simply break my heart.

People sometimes ask how I cope with seeing these things. The truth is that, while I miss my family and my children more than I can say, the hardest part is always returning home, where a whole different reality exists which is, largely, so indifferent to the suffering of humanity in other parts of the world. Many of these poor people would probably give a limb to live in the comfort we enjoy, and with the provision we have. I don't have any words to describe the impact of these people on my understanding of our lives in the UK. The contrast between the two cultures and lifestyles and the huge divide between rich and poor are baffling and incomprehensible. Each time I return from Syria, I leave a part of my heart there.

To me, after living through a terrifying night of rocket attacks in Damascus, after spending time in our hospital serving the poorest people who live in damaged ruins and poverty in Deir ez-Zor, and after sitting with these orphans and widows across Syria who have survived the most appalling atrocities, and who are then forced to send their children out to work in order to eat, much of the materialistic and pleasure-seeking focus that characterises how we live in the UK suddenly seems utterly meaningless. Coffee machines, well-tended gardens, high-definition TVs, huge parties for five-year-olds and exotic holidays seem bizarrely superficial and empty after the simplicity of life and the deprivation I see in parts of Syria.

My beautiful children are an inspiration to me, and I sometimes consider how I would feel if, in years to come, their lives each took very different courses. What if one of them went through the kind of hell the people in Syria have lived through, losing his home many times, his wife or children being brutally killed? What if he and his family had to run for their lives in the night, taking nothing with them, fleeing from armed extremists who would kill them if they caught them? What if they then ended up living in a squalid building shared with other families, or in a tent, struggling to scrape together enough money to eat? And what if, while that was happening, my other son lived a life of comfort, well-fed and happy, seeking to fill his house with beautiful things, and his spare time with fun activities and amazing holidays abroad? I think I have an idea of how I would feel. Heartbroken. Could he really spend his time and money in this way while his brother was suffering so terribly? Couldn't he spare just a little of what he had to improve the life of his brother? I could never have peace if I saw them both living such different realities.

I am sure God feels the same heartbreak when he looks at this world and sees the huge divide between his children: the rich and the poor. Yet many of us in the West who are so rich by these poor people's standards struggle to see it. Many of us feel, somehow, that we don't have anything much to give, not realising that giving even a little of what we have could make all the difference to a family living in the kind of poverty-stricken conditions many families in Syria live in.

Sacrifice means giving to the point of discomfort for the benefit of someone else. I feel that sacrifice is a concept which, in our comfort and complacency, has become rather alien to us in the West. Sacrifice looks different for each of us. For some, the sacrifice may be money or possessions; for others, the sacrifice is time. For many of us, it is both.

Each one of us, as individuals, makes choices each day which determine the course of our own lives here, but which also indirectly determine the course of the lives of others elsewhere. Each one of us has the power to change this world we live in, and if we can't change the world for everyone, then perhaps we could just focus on changing the world for someone.

17

Why a Mother Travels to Syria

Isis Orphans in Deir ez-Zor, May 2018

In Deir ez-Zor I was taught a lesson about generosity and pride by a twelve-year-old orphaned boy. We had bought falafel sandwiches for lunch as they are cheap and, most of all, delicious. As we stood outside the traditional Syrian sweet shop over the road eating our sandwiches, I kept getting tahini sauce around my mouth. The sandwich was too big to eat daintily!

Taking pity on me, the vendors of the falafel stall sent a boy across the road with a handful of tissues. I was touched, as you don't often see service like this in the UK. I thanked the young boy dressed in filthy clothes which may not have seen any water other than rain in months.

We began talking to the boy, who now had no choice but to work to survive. With a shy smile, and eyes projecting an age and wisdom at odds with the size of his small body, he answered our questions. He was one of eight children (a normal number among the big families in this area). The youngest was his brother, aged four, while the rest were sisters up to the age of sixteen. His sisters went to school, but he had finished school now. His father was killed by ISIS, and so, at the age of twelve, this boy was now the 'man of the family'. This was a close Sunni Muslim community with much social etiquette around the behaviour of women and their interactions, especially in situations where they may come into contact with men. It was preferable for the older girls not to go to work alone, nor would it be ideal for the mother, who had the rest of the family to look after, to go out to work. So the responsibility fell on the shoulders of this young boy.

I have seen many examples of this during my times in Syria, but in a climate of dust-settling, wound-licking and feet-finding after years of siege, human rights abuses, trauma and bombing, many extreme practices are to be found in these areas. They are most striking among the youngest members of the community.

On the salary of a runner boy at a falafel stall, which sells one of the cheapest fast foods available, a family of nine just about managed to buy bread. I was so moved. This young man was no longer a child, but was now functioning as an adult with a big burden to carry. He had no chance of an education to build a better life or a brighter future. What was this boy able to hope for in life?

Poverty builds greater poverty. Poverty of education and opportunity is perhaps the most devastating kind of all. In this degree of destitution, the cycle of need and hardship simply fuels itself, and with it comes a range of complex problems stemming from lack of education, lack of hygiene and lack of ability to rise out of the pit of poverty. Without radical intervention, poverty is all this boy's future family will have to look forward to.

The sweet stall was something I had been eyeing up, after promising my own children I would bring them some Syrian sweets. I asked the young boy whether I could buy some for him, but he smiled and refused before returning to his work. Puzzled, we asked the sweet shop keeper if we could buy some for him to give the boy once we had gone.

There was a tap on my arm and I looked round to see the boy at my side, holding a cold can of Pepsi he had just opened, with a straw sticking out. I was both humbled and touched deeply by the generosity of this young boy who had nothing to give, yet still found hospitality in his heart. He was generous to a stranger and, even more, a foreigner. I knew that declining his gift was not an option as I would upset him if I tried to, so I thanked him profusely and began to drink.

Perplexed, but also fascinated and inspired, I listened as I was told that the sweet shop owner knew the boy well, and knew that he would not change his mind about accepting sweets from us. The man explained that this boy was now the son of all of them there and that they all cared for him. As he weighed out an overflowing bag of sweets in shiny wrappers for my children,

I explained that I would like to buy another bag for the boy and his family. The shop owner told me he would give the boy the same sized bag of sweets, but he would not accept any money for them from us.

Now even more baffled, I pondered the fact that I had wanted to do something tiny, not just for the boy, but to also support the local economy, which was slowly starting to be rebuilt after five years of enforced deprivation and neglect. After negotiating with the man, we conceded out of respect for their pride and dignity, and instead bought a bag of dried *molokhia* from the next stall to take home. This encounter left me disappointed, but I also felt something else. I felt stirred and inspired by these amazing people who, despite their great needs, consider themselves able to give more than to receive. I was both humbled and inspired by this experience.

As I discussed the activities of the day with Dr A, I relayed my encounter with this young boy and his community. He explained that the refusal to accept a gift from us was the mentality of the Syrian people as a whole, including the poor people of the country. He recounted a famous Arabic story of a rich but generous man who became poor through giving. He eventually had nothing to his name but a horse, which was his only possession. More importantly, the horse was his livelihood and his only means to earn any income.

He described how this poor man came across a widow with many children and how he had no food to offer them, so he cooked his horse to feed them rather than leave them without offering them hospitality, regardless of the position it left him in. The widow and children had no idea what he had cooked for them, until the next day they saw him leaving on foot rather than with the horse he had arrived on. This may be an extreme illustration, but it goes some way to demonstrating the pride and generosity of the Syrian people.

Dr A went on to explain that the only way for people like this boy and the sweet shop owner to accept a gift from me would be if they felt they were one of my family: that my family were theirs and their family were mine.

As I pondered the day's events and the fascinating and generous culture ingrained in these beautiful people's hearts, I felt that we in the West could learn a great deal about warmth and generosity from these poorest of the poor in Syria.

Another story told by Mother Teresa came to mind, one which had left a big impression on me a few years earlier. When she took a bowl of rice to a family who had not eaten for days, Mother Teresa was surprised to see the mother scoop half of the rice into a different bowl and take it outside. When the mother returned empty-handed, Mother Teresa asked her what she had done with the rice. The mother explained that her neighbours were hungry too, so she had taken some to them. Mother Teresa went on to observe how the wealthy give from their excess, while the poor give from their need.

The poor in these communities give from the fragments they possess, fragments which they are relying on to eat or to survive. In contrast, many of us in the West give only from what we feel we can spare without having to sacrifice anything, and certainly not our next meal. I was reminded of how my mother taught me as I was growing up that no matter how little we have, even if we have only enough food to eat one last meal and no money to buy the next one, we should always be ready to share our last meal with someone in need. This is a principle I have seen her model throughout my life. In times when she has had very little, she has always been willing to put her hand in her pocket to give to someone in need, even if doing so has left her in a difficult position.

I was surprised when I arrived in Deir ez-Zor to be told that, before the war, a stranger could knock on the door of someone and ask to stay the night. The residents of the house would then vacate their home and stay somewhere else, so that the stranger could have their space and their privacy, and they would not accept a penny in return for this sacrifice. I feel this is what Jesus was talking about when he spoke of us welcoming strangers into our home.

Dr A explained that this difference in our understanding of what generosity and community look like is one of the reasons most western missionaries fail in this kind of environment. They come with their western understanding of giving which in the West may seem generous. But in Syria they fail to make a true impression on these enormously generous people, who will give to their own ruin in an effort to show kindness and hospitality. While this story may be extreme, I ask myself how many of us in the West would cook our horse to show hospitality to a stranger or to feed a family who were hungry?

So the next day I went to visit orphans and widows in Deir ez-Zor with a Syrian attitude towards generosity and hospitality, ready to adopt new sisters, sons and daughters into my own family, and to be a sister and mother to the women and children I met that day.

There was one family we had given aid to, which I visited, and who I will never forget. Our team had interviewed the father during our large aid distributions, before he was later killed. His seven-year-old son had been killed when an ISIS fighter ran him over and did not stop to help him. In the video our team took of the man telling his story, his young stepdaughter sat on the floor bottle feeding his newborn baby, and listening again to the wretched events which had cost him parts of his body.

He described how ISIS had demanded al zakat taxes from all people in the area, but instead of using the money to care for those who were poor, they used it to support their fighters and their families. He spoke of how ISIS took all their food and kept it in large storehouses and covered pits dug in the desert while the people and their children in the area went hungry. He struggled to find work during the siege and became unable to feed his family.

Watching his children suffer from hunger drove him to desperation, and he dared to steal a bag of flour from one of the ISIS storehouses in the desert. No more than five kilograms, he told our team. Just one bag to make bread for his starving family.

A few days later he was arrested and beaten from head to foot. He was put in a tiny cell around one metre by one metre in size. He was hung from the ceiling by his hands, blindfolded, tortured and beaten for four or five days with no food. After this he was taken to one of the ISIS courts.

He was forced to his knees, where he was flogged with a leather whip. After a 'trial' with no legal representation, and with the verdict having been decided beforehand, he was taken to an underground medical centre in a school. There his right hand and left foot were cut off above the wrist and ankle. He described how they hit his leg repeatedly to break the bones. It was utterly incomprehensible, and yet this story is not an isolated one.

Sometimes people ask why, as a mother of two young boys, I risk my life to go to a place like Syria as it has been one of the most dangerous and complex war zones in the world. This is why. As a mother, my heartfelt prayer is that someone, somewhere, would be willing to do the same for my children if the situation was reversed. We are called to treat others the way we want to be treated.

In Deir ez-Zor I also visited two young orphaned boys and their grandmother. As we sat in the small first-floor apartment sipping *ahway*, the grandmother recounted their gut-wrenching story. Two and a half years before, the boys had been travelling with their parents from Deir ez-Zor, where ISIS was in control, to Latakia to visit their maternal grandmother. Their car was stopped by ISIS fighters. They were taken to an ISIS prison because their mother came from Latakia. ISIS didn't like this as it indicated she was a Shia Muslim rather than a Sunni. The father was separated from the mother and children, and they were all put in prison. The mother was beaten in front of her children, and they watched her being whipped until she had wounds which bled into the night. These little children had to watch this happen to their mother, completely powerless to do anything to help her or stop what they were seeing. For months they endured torture and abuse, both physical and psychological.

After six months, their jailers put them all in the same room, and the parents wept as they said goodbye to their children, telling them they were about to be killed, but the children would be set free. They told their children they had done nothing wrong to deserve these executions, and that the boys should try to go and be happy and live a good life.

The children were beside themselves and became hysterical, crying and wailing loudly. The jailers told the older boy that if they didn't shut up, they would be killed with their parents. The boys had every reason to believe them. Their paternal grandmother in Deir ez-Zor received a call saying her grandsons would be left in Al-Hasakeh, the neighbouring governorate. If she wanted them, she shouldn't waste any time as they would be left there alone. She arrived to find them wandering the streets, distressed. They were filthy, their clothes were torn, and their hair had grown long and was infested with head lice.

She took them back to their family home in Deir ez-Zor, but she quickly decided they couldn't stay there. The boys were psychologically paralysed and damaged by their traumatic experiences, and many things in their home seemed to trigger their tears and emotions. Everything reminded these children of their parents, and they would search out their mother's and father's clothes, hugging them at night until they fell asleep. She rented an apartment to try to start a new chapter in their lives. But these boys were simply unable to turn to the next page.

In the beginning they had lost any ability to care for their own hygiene and had to be taught all over again. Even now, two years on, she still had to help them get washed. They were engulfed in a deep depression and were unable to eat normally. The grandmother described how it would sometimes take hours to finish a meal because they would have to be prompted to take each mouthful or even to chew each mouthful. She described them as being like machines.

The younger boy lost all interest in life and social interaction, instead sitting alone staring into space. While I sat with them, I watched as he gazed listlessly at the floor. When his neighbour spoke softly with him, he looked at her, yet seemed unable to respond or give coherent answers. He was attending school, but he could not integrate. His teachers tried to encourage him to play with the other children, but he usually chose to sit alone instead.

The older boy, who was now thirteen, had suffered even more since this ordeal. In an attempt to distract him from his memories, as well as to cover the costs of living, his family found him a job assisting a mechanic fixing cars. But the man he worked for beat him, a thirteen-year-old boy who had already suffered more than any young child should ever have to suffer. The grandmother was now unwilling to send him out to work again. She feared that because he was psychologically damaged and unable to interact with people on a normal level, his vulnerability would be taken advantage of.

The children still woke at night crying and shouting, and their grandmother took to locking their door as she had found them sleepwalking, and was worried about them hurting themselves. She also described how they fought viciously with each other, leaving marks on each other's skin. They must have witnessed and directly experienced horrific examples of violence during the six months they spent with ISIS. With repeated exposure to violence, a child is quickly conditioned to behave in a violent way.

After meeting this desperately sad family, I asked myself how a mother would ever cope after the murder of her son and daughter-in-law. How could two young boys return to any kind of normal life after six months in an ISIS prison, being beaten and watching their mother being savagely tortured before both of their parents were callously murdered? How could a grandmother, with her own array of health problems, care for two orphaned boys for whom the word 'traumatised' brings a whole new meaning?

These are enormous questions with no easy answers, but I believe the most important thing is love, and it simply has to start somewhere. After the grandmother had told me their painful and horror-filled story, I asked her a question. I hesitated, as it was a tough and seemingly insensitive question. But I also felt it was important. I asked what her hopes were for the future for her grandsons.

After all the terrible things we had talked about that morning, this was the question which broke her. She sat silently for the first time since we arrived, slowly taking off her glasses to wipe away her tears. The atmosphere in the room filled with people was suddenly intense in the silence, and I couldn't stop my own tears from flowing as I went to sit beside her on the floor.

Even Haitham, who was translating and who had visited many families with me before, dabbed his own eyes with tissues as the grandmother and I wept on each other's shoulders.

It was the watershed moment in our meeting, and the point at which we moved from composed to vulnerable, from professional to intimate, and from sitting politely on the sofa to getting down on the floor to hold and hug and share with them in their suffering. True trust is not something that can be built from a distance, and genuine love is not something that can be demonstrated at arm's length. Real and unconditional love is something that is up close and personal.

Many of us in the West need to allow our hearts to be broken by the injustice these people have been dealt. Personally, I was not ready or motivated to go out of my way to give more than just a standard response – until my heart was broken by what I saw happening in the Middle East. Providing meaningful support in such a complex environment as Syria is something that takes time, commitment, perseverance and organisation. The heartbreak I felt after Jesus gave me the ability to see more from God's perspective was the call to action I needed to respond in the first place, and then to maintain the stamina to keep going.

Deir ez-Zor is a place where everyone has suffered and has lived under the control of al-Nusra and then ISIS. It is not something unique to a minority of people, it is something which has affected everyone. Although an estimated one to two hundred thousand people had, by this point, returned to the city since its liberation, much of its population had lived through the savagery and had seen brutal punishments carried out publicly, with some having been forced to watch executions. Everyone had a story to tell.

Whether I was talking with the man in the bakery or with the employees in our hospital, they had seen and lived through the very worst crimes of which humanity is capable. This suffering was not just isolated to the widow and her two fatherless children, or to the widow I had visited the night before. In Deir ez-Zor, and in many other parts of Syria that were under siege, this trauma and suffering was not the exception, it was the rule.

I hesitated to take pictures of these beautiful boys as it is the part of this work I hate, but the grandmother was insistent. She wanted the world to know what they have suffered, what Syria has suffered, and she hoped that the people and entities who fund and support these terrorist groups will see what they have created, and the life-changing effect their evil actions have had on the innocent children who should be protected and nurtured at all costs.

Once again, I was deeply moved by the Syrian spirit of generosity and kindness. This widowed grandmother who had suffered so much and who was already relying on support to survive would not let me leave without promising that, next time I came, I would sleep in her house, so that she could cook for me. We hugged and kissed, and kissed and hugged again. It is impossible not to fall in love with these people who are so vulnerable, yet so warm and open-handed. Even many of the worst-affected show the most inspiring resilience.

This is why I travel to Syria. These children are precious, and are just as valuable in God's eyes as my children. They have needs just as much as mine do. I may not be able to help all of the children in Syria, but I pray we will be able to make a difference to the ones God puts in front of us.

As a child, my worst fear was for one of my parents to die. I remember feeling terrified by the prospect. For these two boys, every child's worst nightmare became their reality. If the situation were reversed, I would hope there would be someone willing to cross land and sea to do something to help my children. If this is what we would want in our hearts if we weren't here to care for our own children, then isn't it our human responsibility to do something proactive to help children like these?

Rebuilding hopes and hearts takes time, commitment and perseverance, but most of all, it takes love. Actions speak louder than words, but the two work beautifully in tandem to show the unconditional love of God to the broken, hurting, poor and vulnerable. Our work is built on the love and actions of many, to bring relief to the most vulnerable in Syria.

18

Taking Counsel from the Lord

Spring and Summer 2018

After we opened our small field hospital in the rubble of Deir ez-Zor, we were offered a partnership by an individual with resources and connections. It seemed like an amazing opportunity. I felt at the time that perhaps we should stop and pray about whether this partnership was from God. Foolishly, I brushed this feeling aside, asking myself how it could be anything but a gift. As the weeks passed, however, we started to feel that this individual's motivations were not the same as ours, and we began to feel uneasy.

One day, while I was bringing the children home from school, my mind was occupied by this project. As I walked through the front door, the words 'do not be unequally yoked together with unbelievers' from 2 Corinthians 6:14 came to mind. This person was not a follower of Jesus. Yet, I once again found myself unwisely brushing aside this warning from the Holy Spirit, instead trying to justify this partnership by telling myself that they had faith, just a different faith to us. More importantly, they had seemed willing to give to help the poorest and most vulnerable. Surely serving the poor had been at the heart of Jesus?

Over time, however, we became increasingly frustrated with the situation, as this person was just not showing the commitment we had expected. A couple of weeks later, the night before Good Friday, I had a disturbing dream which we had trouble interpreting at the time. The one thing clear in this dream was that there was something developing which could threaten our work.

We prayed about my dream and tried to understand its

meaning, as it had definitely felt like a warning relating to our work. We asked God whether it was connected with this person and project, as the thought had crossed my mind.

A few weeks later, in May, I was in Syria. Before I left for Deir ez-Zor, Dr A and I prayed early in the morning. We didn't know what to expect from my first visit there. It was still such a volatile area, under tight military control, and there were still pockets of ISIS, and fighting in parts of the governorate. It wasn't easy to gain permission for me to visit the area, and one of the concerns was kidnapping, as this is how many of the jihadist groups and criminal gangs make money. Travelling along empty desert roads leaves people extremely vulnerable, and a western woman would be an easy target. We prayed for guidance, then opened the Bible.

The passage it opened at was from Ezra, chapter 9. It described how the Israelites had intermarried with foreign women who worshipped other gods and idols. God had forbidden them from intermarrying, as it would end with them falling away from the one true God who loved them unconditionally, to instead serve idols and gods who had no love for them, nor any power to help or guide them, and in doing so develop unhealthy behaviours. Yet they had disobediently married, and even had children, with these foreign men and women.

We were too blind to understand the significance of this passage, and didn't know what to make of it at the time. I didn't understand it until seven months later, when we did remember to take counsel from the Lord before considering a partnership with another organisation in Syria. They were also not followers of Jesus, but they were a good, genuine and trustworthy organisation who had worked alongside our team to distribute some of our aid. I have great respect for them. They were very different from the person we had struggled with before, but it was clear to us that God did not want us to commit to a long-term partnership or 'marriage' with them on the medical project they had offered, as it would leave us at their mercy, and not in full control of the project. It would not lift up the name of Jesus.

While I was still in Syria on that visit in May, we began to feel more uncomfortable about the initial partnership we were offered. I am ashamed to say it took us so long, but after I returned we sat down to pray intensely over the situation, and to truly seek God's guidance as to how to handle it. Dr A and I prayed from the heart. We were led to a passage in the Bible which taught an important lesson about the consequences of making assumptions. I realised how gracious and patient God had been with me over this situation, as we had made many assumptions about getting involved with a partnership that appeared to be a great blessing without having prayed about it first.

The next day, I went to a Bible study. On that day we happened to be studying the book of Joshua. As we discussed chapter 9, the passage where the Gibeonites made a peace treaty with the men of Israel, it struck a chord with me about our situation. The whole chapter felt significant, but the words which resonated were in verse 14, where it said the men of Israel were deceived into making a peace treaty with the Gibeonites because they 'did not ask counsel from the LORD' (ESV).

On the one hand, a 'humanitarian' perspective would say the men of Israel had been deceived by the Gibeonites so it wasn't their fault, and they made a peace treaty with them, which surely must be a good thing. But a Christian perspective would say that if they had taken counsel from the Lord before making this agreement, God would have steered them away from this deception, and they wouldn't have entered into an agreement which they couldn't reverse, and which would have devastating long-term consequences. God's vision goes further than ours, into the future, and he sees every situation from a different angle, from which we don't have the ability to see things.

Sometimes we have to make difficult decisions and walk away from situations which look attractive or beneficial because the long-term consequences will not be good, even if they look fantastic now. This is what ultimately happened for the Israelites who were tricked into making a peace treaty which God didn't want them to make. Ultimately we, too, were led along by what seemed like a good opportunity but which turned out not to be. More importantly, after we walked away from this potential partnership, over time we saw clearly that it would have been a big mistake for us to commit to it. We breathed a sigh of relief that we had got off so lightly before binding ourselves to a commitment we would have struggled to get out of.

The Sunday after studying Joshua 9, I went up for prayer at the end of our church service. I hadn't said anything to the woman who came up to pray for me, as I prefer to let the Holy Spirit lead our prayers. We knew each other, though, and she was very involved with our church. Although she had supported our appeals when we ran them at church, she was not actively involved at any other time and I had not publicly shared the story of how God gave us the vision for Grace (Jerusalem) Hospital by showing us the passages in Zechariah 1, 2 and 4 a year before. I had not told the story to more than a handful of people. Yet as she prayed for me, she said, 'I pray Samara will return to the plumb line.'

I wondered if I had heard her correctly. She had no way at all of knowing the significance of the passage in Zechariah 4 to our work in Syria the year before, especially verse 10, where it says, 'Do not despise these small beginnings, for the LORD rejoices to see the work begin, to see the plumb line in Zerubbabel's hand' (NLT).

The potential partnership and the projects that came with it had been a huge distraction from our bigger vision of designing and building a larger hospital. Was God telling us now to focus more on this big project?

When the woman had finished praying, I asked her whether she had really said 'plumb line'. She looked a little embarrassed as she said yes. I asked her why, and she appeared to be unsure. She said that she had never said the words 'plumb line' before!

I was amazed. When God first gave us this passage around a year ago, the small verse about Zerubbabel with the plumb line in his hand had been enormously significant and we had spent a lot of time discussing it, as well as the meaning and function of the plumb line. It had seemed especially relevant to what we were doing at the time in relation to our big hospital project.

The woman had spoken these words without thinking and without understanding what she was saying or why. I believe she was guided by the Holy Spirit to say those words, and God was giving me the instruction, through her; first, to return to our big hospital vision, and second, to ensure that our approach was always using God as our 'vertical reference, or measure' for big decisions. At this time, we were still waiting for the final planning permission for this hospital, and it took another six months to get it.

The Bible has been a continuing source of guidance for me – not just at those moments when I have felt I had a big decision to make, but each day. Every day I am amazed by something new I have understood in this phenomenal book, or understood in a different light. The free 'Bible in One Year' app has been a great resource for me and I use it most days. I have also introduced Dr A to this wonderful tool. It is a great encouragement to him too. Where he is in Syria, he is surrounded by many people of Christian heritage, but not by a community of believers actively seeking Jesus, and this app has been a great encouragement to him each day. Personally, I prefer to read the passages and commentaries each day from my phone. As he is not a native English speaker, Dr A prefers to press 'play' and to listen to both the Bible passages and the commentaries being read to him. These nuggets of inspiration have been a fantastic way to start or boost each day, and everyone I know who uses this app or who receives the updates as emails gains great encouragement from it.

19

Worth More than Sparrows

Autumn 2018

The boy grinned proudly at me as he held out his wiry arm with something dangling from his hand. My face fell as I saw what looked like a dead bird hanging upside down from his fingers. The boy's clothes were dirty, and his face was no cleaner. He giggled as the bird suddenly flapped its wings, causing him to snatch it back between both hands. Gasping, I watched as he manhandled the tiny feathered form with a general lack of concern for the well-being of this defenceless creature. It was his now, and he could do what he liked with it. His friends laughed and excitedly tossed instructions at him, bemused by my alarm over the fate of the small sparrow.

'Look!' I said in my basic Arabic, hurrying to open the car door and then rummaging for the box of granola I had brought in my hand luggage. Tearing open the box, I grabbed a handful of dried cereal and held it out for the bird. The boys looked on in fascination as the oldest of them pointed the bird down towards the grains in the palm of my hand. The bird's neck was rigid, and it remained stiff and unresponsive. It was frozen with terror.

'He will die!' I persisted with my limited language capabilities. I looked up at the old man who was watching, intrigued, but unmoved by the possible fate of the little bird. Like the boys, he didn't speak a word of English, so I called out to my driver, whose English was perhaps on a par with my Arabic, appealing to him to tell the boys to let it go. He barely grunted as his eyes and hands remained fixed on his phone. Clearly it was up to me with my restricted communication skills.

'Here,' I beckoned to the boys, patting a concrete ledge on

the side of a building. No sooner had the boy relaxed his fingers than the bird flapped its way to safety under the nearest parked car. I breathed a sigh of relief as it was now at least out of reach of the overzealous boys with a heavy-handed approach to entertainment. After pressing their cheeks to the ground and throwing stones at the shaken bird under the car for a few minutes, they turned their attention to my questions. After our introductions, the smaller of the three boys, Nader, announced that his older friend didn't speak. 'He can listen, but he doesn't talk,' he told me.

I asked if they went to school. '*Marfi madrassi* [No school],' was the reply. Instead, they hung around the immigration office at the Syrian border and around the checkpoints on either side to pass the time, perhaps hoping for a little attention. A small crowd had gathered around us by now.

'Would you like something to eat?' I asked. Their innocent smiles and tentative nods sent me back to the car, this time for a pack of Bourbon biscuits I had brought for my host family. As I opened the pack and handed out biscuits, they politely declined at first, looking shy. But without too much persuasion they soon reached out their hands to take the chocolate biscuits. Placing the rest of the packet into little Nader's hand, I said they were for all their friends. As they ran off, with Nader clutching the pack, I escaped from the stifling heat into the air-conditioned car.

Eight hours had passed since I arrived at the border, and many prayers had been said during this time for the officer in charge to issue my visa. But perhaps this was one of those occasions when I was praying the wrong prayer, because God gives us what we need, even if not what we ask for or want.

While I had been sitting in the familiar Syrian arrivals lounge earlier that morning, I met other people struggling to get in, as well as to get out. The room was adorned with no fewer than twenty assorted posters of Bashar al-Assad and some ragged bunting, half of which was made up of tatty Syrian flags, and the other half of smaller pictures of the president. Large sheets of grubby paint flaked off the walls behind rusty radiators.

Mismatched energy-saving light bulbs dangled from the ill-fitting original lights which hung loosely from the ceiling.

A nervous teenage boy dressed in dirty clothes scampered out from the offices behind the front desks, holding a wastepaper basket, as an older man issued instructions embellished by animated hand gestures. Sweeping the floor with his bare hands, then picking up the rubbish, the boy looked back over his shoulder occasionally to check he was doing the right thing. I smiled warmly at him as he approached my patch of the floor.

Having been told that no one with a UK or US passport could gain a visa on the border now, our team had been trying hard all day to call in favours. But in the extremely tense political climate around Idlib, and amid the threats issued by western governments, together with other tensions that simmered behind the scenes, it appeared that favours were not available that day. One of our team had visited this same immigration office the day before with all our documents and had been given the OK for today. But as is often the case in Syria, something had changed overnight.

There had also been a change in climate recently for foreign spouses of Syrian nationals. On this day, another foreign woman had arrived with her Syrian husband but had not been granted access with him, and yet another foreign woman had arrived with her two sons of Syrian nationality without her Syrian husband. She had met with the same fate. Her distress was evident as her sons tried hard to console her.

In spite of my frustration, I also understood the suspicions aroused by foreigners in such a complex war zone. Throughout this war, the nations and entities who supported various parties involved in the conflict had used many means to get people into Syria. Marriage and humanitarian aid were two very obvious ways. There were many reported instances over the years, but I had been deeply troubled the year before to hear an account of a Syrian woman who had married a foreign man.

They had lived in Syria and had young children together. The foreign husband had been involved in humanitarian work and was respected in the community. But all who knew them had been shaken when both the man and his wife were arrested. He was reported to have been in Syria under cover, employed by a foreign intelligence agency to work his way through an assassination list of high-ranking Syrian officials. The man escaped from prison, but his wife did not. Whether she knew of his true motives or not, no one knew. But those poor children had been brought into this world on the basis of a lie. I could barely imagine how these impressionable souls could begin to make sense of their existence, given the dysfunctional façade of the family into which they had been born. Why were they here, and could they trust anyone at all in this broken world if not their own father?

I had spent the day alternating between sitting in the sparse arrivals lounge, or the air-conditioned car and wandering around making occasional, basic conversations with anyone patient or bored enough to listen to my fragmented attempts to speak Arabic.

Now, as I sat in the car, the old man who had watched my earlier interaction with the boys and the bird knocked on the car window. He held out a tiny cup of the traditional strong black Arabic coffee that is usually mixed in with a large volume of thick and murky coffee grounds. I gave him a smile of gratitude as it had been such a long and exhausting twenty-four hours. Syrian hospitality is dependable and generous. I might not have been given a visa, but the old man, who worked in the office, was nevertheless reinforcing this precious cultural tradition.

Another hour passed before my fate was finally confirmed. I would not be entering Syria today. Although I had realised by now that this would be the most likely outcome, I had clung on to a little hope as I had nothing to lose by continuing to wait. This news was sorely disappointing. We had made many plans for this short visit, and I had had a busy schedule arranged.

Without a Syrian embassy in the UK, applying for a visa in advance from outside the country was not easy. My three previous visits had been made possible through gaining a visa on the border. The visas having been granted because of my work in sending aid to the Syrian people, as well as because of the trust our team in Syria had in me and the lack of a Syrian embassy in the UK. But now there was a new clampdown on foreigners, especially British or American, entering the country without a visa having been arranged in advance.

Deflated, we set off for Beirut again. Despite its own charm, I had hoped not to see that city for another week. I thanked God that the most important part of my trip to Beirut had been completed earlier in the day. That, after all, had been my main reason for coming to the Middle East this time, but it had seemed a missed opportunity not to venture into Syria to visit our projects and have some meetings while in the area. But we felt that God, in his wisdom, had a good reason that we could not see, for not allowing me into Syria this time.

The next day, I wandered down to the tiny patch of sand between the rocks on the shoreline next to the main high road running through Beirut. I sat on a boulder as the glowing orange sun sank slowly into the sea, and watched people casting and winding in fishing lines. These people weren't fishing for sport, they were fishing for their needs. After a while, two little girls appeared, confident and chatty, and beckoned me to come and climb over the rocks to the other side where their 'Babba' was fishing.

As I picked up my shoes which I had removed to dip my feet in the warm waves, one of the little girls persistently tried to encourage me to follow them over the rocks. Not feeling so nimble, I declined before translating some little notes my oldest son had written for me before I left England. The girls were taken with the messages saying he loved me, written on glittery-backed wrapping paper. After looking through the photos on my phone, the oldest girl picked up a sandy dead fish which had washed up on the shore, holding it out to me between her thumb and forefinger.

Once again, I politely declined, explaining that I was staying in a hotel and couldn't cook it. I asked where they were from. 'Darayya,' came her reply. Syria. So many Syrian children were also now facing a life of inequality and uncertainty in Lebanon, as well as in other countries. Syrians now made up a third of the population in Lebanon. Lebanese law restricted Syrian refugees from taking on anything other than menial employment, and many struggled even to find that. The oversaturated labour market drove down the wages, not only for the Syrian refugees trying to feed their families, but also for the poorer Lebanese population, causing tension between the host and refugee communities. It was a lose–lose situation for all of the poorest there, regardless of their nationality.

As I crossed over the busy high road in the Beirut evening rush hour, it was amazing to watch the six lanes of traffic travelling in each direction. The absence of road markings among so many lines of traffic, exacerbated by the scarcity of working traffic lights, was no doubt part of the reason for the insistent hoots and beeps against the background of engines on this busy road. Walking back to my hotel, I couldn't help but draw parallels between the Syrian people, both inside and outside Syria, and the little sparrow I had seen being tormented by those boys who simply knew no better.

So many Syrians had learnt to dodge snipers, bombs and the many enemies they had faced in their own neighbourhoods, homes and workplaces. They were not so very different from the traumatised little bird, bruised and battered under the car, trying to take a moment's pause for breath. All they needed was a chance to recover, and the hope that the perpetrators of their misery would be distracted by something else instead and leave them alone.

It reminded me of the passage in the Bible where Jesus was hanging on the cross, brutalised, bloody, tortured and stripped of all dignity. At that moment, Jesus, in his innocence, had every right to feel indignant and angry and to place blame. But instead he chose to intercede for his tormentors, asking our Father in heaven simply to 'forgive them, for they don't know what they are doing' (Luke 23:34 NLT).

In the same way, those boys had continued with their game, fixated on the little bird, yet understanding nothing, and caring little about the impact they were having on a life which seemed so insignificant and worthless to them. They also had no idea what they were doing. Or perhaps they had an idea that what they were doing was wrong yet enjoyed the feeling of power they had over this bird. Or perhaps they gained a kick out of watching the little bird suffer. They acted in ignorance.

Likewise, the perpetrators of the war in Syria seem ignorant of, or disinterested in, the destruction and suffering they have caused, caring little for the vulnerable lives of the voiceless people who seem so small, insignificant and expendable to them. When, in an entity's or a government's thinking, does the collateral damage involved in achieving a political goal cross the line from an acceptable loss to unjustifiable and wanton massacre and evil?

Those with the biggest, heaviest boots can crush many of the small countries, their culture and their people with just one footstep, as if those people were ants. Yet these tiny and hard-working creatures have an admirable ability to pick themselves up and begin rebuilding their colony as soon as it is damaged. They do not sit and wallow in the crisis of their loss, but rather start working again at the first opportunity. The Syrians show the same resilience, as well as inspiring inner strength to keep going, keep living, keep rebuilding. They simply need, like the little bird under the car, some space, respite and protection, and for the perpetrators of this war to turn their focus away from them, enabling the Syrians to begin to rebuild their neighbourhoods, their homes, their country and their lives.

A few days later, the area in Syria in which I had been due to stay for one night of my trip came under heavy missile attack, on the night I had arranged to stay there. Some of our team were messaging me as it happened. They had had an immensely traumatic night. While they had lived through some of the worst fighting in the conflict before, they had since then become used to a calmer environment and had begun to feel safer. They had felt, until this attack, that they were now in a place of refuge. Had I been granted a visa at the border a few days before, I would have experienced this violent attack.

I felt that perhaps God had not wanted me to be there for

that terrifying ordeal, and I felt an awkward gratitude for not having had to experience another distressing night under bombardment like the one I had spent in Damascus four months before. But I also felt terribly guilty for feeling this. Some of our team, with families that included young children, had had to endure this nightmare. The Syrian people, likewise, had no other option, no escape route, no safe homes to go back to. This had been the injustice of life in Syria for years now.

One month later, my visa was granted from the Ministry of Interior, and we made plans for my next visit to Syria.

20

Living Under Siege

Speaking Out for the Voiceless, November 2018

It was an unusual sight. The boy clung to his father. His arms were wrapped purposefully around the man's waist as they sat on a thin mat on the floor. They had been sitting like this for the last twenty minutes as we talked. I was reminded of the way my six-year-old had wrapped his arms around my leg a few days earlier as I was leaving for the airport. He had begged me not to go, and his open vulnerability had made our goodbye so much harder.

Here in western Ghouta, the boy who sat in front of me now had assumed this equally needy pose. But this boy was not six – he was sixteen years old. Never before had I seen a sixteen-year-old boy display such close physical affection towards his father in front of strangers. But perhaps this close physical intimacy in the presence of outsiders was an attempt to regain some feelings of reassurance and safety which had been so elusive over the recent years.

The boy's mother had wiped a steady stream of tears from her cheeks as she told us how some of the jihadist fighters controlling their area had been their neighbours. They had joined the groups controlling these areas, who had paid them to fight with them. She told me how they dragged her son around by his hair and subjected him to regular beatings and humiliation. Yet the only hospitals nearby, she said, were for the fighters. When they had tried to seek medical help for their boy for his injuries they had been turned away. They were not welcome, as they were not linked to al-Nusra, which was controlling the area.

Civilians like them who refused to support this internationally proscribed terrorist organisation, were treated very differently to the people who were willing to submit to their leadership, support them, work for them and fight for them. The father had refused to accept this group, and both he and his family had paid an extremely high price for his dissidence. Survival was a daily struggle, with difficulties in finding employment or food.

As I sat crossed-legged on the floor, I felt a sudden cold sensation on my back. We were sitting in the living room of this simple house, but there had been heavy rain that morning. The second drip on my back confirmed that the roof of this poor family's house was leaking.

The mother rubbed her face on her sleeve as we continued to talk. The boy would have been around ten years old when this group took control of their neighbourhood, yet these jihadists had mercilessly attacked and beaten him, leaving him with permanent deformities. He could no longer walk.

The tears his mother shed throughout our meeting were a ceaseless outpouring of her family's pain. Soon after my arrival in their humble home, she emptied out her heart to us, telling us how this group had kidnapped her, keeping her hostage for ten days. They took all her valuable possessions and jewellery. She pushed up her sleeves to reveal the pale scar tissue on her arms, where she told us these 'dogs', as she called them, had poured acid on her, burning her skin.

The father continued when the mother could talk no more, telling us the people who did these things were still living in their neighbourhood. They stayed when some of the other jihadists had left as the siege was broken. His burning anger at the injustice and torture they had suffered was evident as he told us how those 'animals' did not deserve to live.

We gave a wheelchair to their son and new winter shoes and boots to all the children in the house. They are all living in poverty now. Like most people in those newly freed areas, they had no obvious means of work. Over time, some kind of economy would begin to be rebuilt, but in those early days the entire remaining community was still reeling from having experienced such life-changing ordeals. These people were trying to recover from the years of neglect, trauma and hate they had lived through.

By the end of our visit we were all hugging and kissing, and the family were smiling, happy and encouraged when we said our emotional and heartfelt goodbyes. I told them they were strong and courageous people who are an inspiration to us. I told them many of us are praying for them, and for true and lasting peace in their country. They shared a part of their souls with me that day, which I will never forget. I left with a certainty that they had felt heard, seen and valued, and they had felt loved.

Later the same morning, between downpours, we visited another family in a nearby area of Ghouta that had also been under siege. It was unbelievable to think that anyone could live where they did. Especially a disabled lady: the grandmother. The huge piles of rubble made it hard to access her house, but we climbed over them to get a wheelchair and Zimmer frame to her.

During the siege her house was partially destroyed too, and every room upstairs was affected by fire damage. Thick black soot coated all the ceilings, and every window was without glass. The kitchen had an enormous gaping hole in the wall made by a bomb, and there were puddles of rainwater on all the floors, in the hallway, lounge and kitchen. It had poured with rain that morning, and the evidence was all over the house.

The grandmother told me that during the siege the al-Nusra fighters had come to their home and lined up all fifteen members of her family, including the children, in the middle of the night. They were about to start killing them one by one, but something happened to distract the fighters, giving the family the chance to escape in their pyjamas. They went to Quneitra, where they stayed for a year. They then had to flee again when their new home was bombed.

They had returned to this house in Ghouta in the last couple of months. It had been taken during the fighting by one of the families connected with al-Nusra, who had made it their home

for the time this area was under siege. In the fight to break the
siege it had been bombed and much of it burnt. Since then, a
huge amount of work had been done to get the ground floor
habitable again, although I'm sure most British people would
consider the big puddles on the floor and the holes in the roof
and walls to be completely unacceptable living conditions for
any human. How could a family of fifteen, with small children
and a disabled grandmother who sits on the floor all day, live
there in the winter?

The mobility items were essential for the old lady, and the
little children needed the wellies just to keep their feet dry and
warm *inside* the house during the wet and cold months. The
shoes and boots brought smiles to all the family, and once again,
we left them as though we were leaving our own relatives.
Sometimes it is the little things which make a big difference.

A few days before, I had visited a widow now living in Latakia
with her three daughters. They used to live in Shtabraq, in Idlib.
One night while she and her family were sleeping, al-Nusra
fighters had come, killing the residents of this village in their
homes and even in their beds. She said these fighters had been
hiding in caves, in fields and underground until the night they
struck and took control of the village. The people I met said
around a thousand al-Nusra fighters arrived with guns and
bombs.

Many villagers ran away just in time, but they said hundreds
were killed and they described bombs coming down like rain.
Many of the victims' throats were cut when this attack took
place in April 2015. They killed the father of these three girls.
He was not a soldier or a fighter, just an ordinary person. But
the jihadists killed him anyway, taking the rest of the family as
prisoners. The mother had to try to run up a ramp with her
children while trying to escape, but the terror she felt made her
incapable and she fell three times while trying to get up it.

One of her neighbours watched her thirteen-year-old daughter
being shot. She briefly held her in her arms as she was dying,
but had to abandon her precious daughter as she was breathing
her last breaths in order to try to save her son. But he was still

taken by the jihadists. Some of the women were also taken by them and were forced to 'marry' some of the fighters. They were thought to have been taken to other countries.

This widow from Shtabraq and her children were all put in prison. The youngest was just five years old at the time, and the oldest had a medical condition. They kept these little and unwell children in prison. The mother described how she was given sixty-five lashes with a leather whip. What could a simple newly widowed mother of four have done to deserve this punishment? After nine months they were set free as part of a negotiated deal to release al-Nusra members the Syrian government had in prison in return for releasing these women and children al-Nusra had been keeping. The widow commented that most of the al-Nusra fighters they encountered were not Syrian, but from other countries. She wept as she spoke of the fear and suffering they had lived through, and of how she still wakes screaming because of nightmares. She cannot forget. One of her daughters has disabilities, but her other children go to school.

So many displaced people flocked to Latakia because of its relative safety compared with other parts of the country. The schools are overcrowded, and the children have to attend in two shifts. Some children do the morning shift of learning, while others do the afternoon.

While her daughters are at school in the afternoon, this widow uses the opportunity to take on poorly paid farming work to try to cover the rent of the one room they all live in. It barely seems worthy of the high rent she has to pay for it, with paint peeling off the damp patches creeping up each of the walls. She simply cannot earn enough to support her four children.

What this woman and her children have been through is simply too much. No child should ever be imprisoned, to be used as a bargaining chip for the release of prisoners linked with a proscribed terrorist organisation.

Widows like this in Syria desperately need support. We gave each of this widow's children a new pair of shoes or boots to help see them through winter. I tried to offer encouragement to this courageous mother raising her children in such difficult circumstances, after everything they have been through.

On the same day I met another widow from the same area in Idlib. She said that both she and her mother-in-law had also been imprisoned by al-Nusra. The elderly grandmother described how she had been kept in prison, and how her grandson had been one of five boys of around twelve years old who had been taken from their families by al-Nusra, taught the Qur'an and taught to fight, while being provided with money. The grandmother spoke of how, over time, these boys had been brainwashed against their own families, whom they now called 'infidels'. She said one of the boys had threatened to kill his grandfather for not following their radical ideology.

These stories are just a couple of examples among an ocean of monstrocities committed in Syria over recent years, and amid a world of affliction endured by ordinary people. The amount of healing needed goes so much further than the physical wounds and disabilities which so many are left with, though the emotional and psychological wounds take longer and are often harder to heal. The amount of unconditional love and forgiveness needed to restore and rebuild communities and lives is infinite, and an equal amount of endurance and commitment are needed to persevere amid all of this pain.

These are the voices of the fragile and vulnerable people in Syria which have been drowned out by the gratuitous propaganda of war. Too much attention has been given to serving a political agenda, and not enough to the real people and their genuine suffering and needs. We are called to care for the orphans and the widows, to speak up for those who cannot speak for themselves. We are called to speak up and judge fairly, to defend the rights of the poor and needy. To keep quiet is to condone what has taken place, but to speak out is to challenge these crimes against humanity which have been committed in our lifetimes, in our generation, and on our watch.

21

Healthcare in Syria

November 2018

As I looked at the incubator, I realised what I was seeing. There was not one baby in this incubator, but two. Both babies were bundled up in pink blankets under the plastic cover.

'They are not twins,' I was told. 'They have different mothers.' I frowned as I digested this. Two babies from different families, two different health problems. But they were in the same incubator, in a hospital room crammed with adult patients.

In Syria, dignity in healthcare is a luxury many people can no longer afford. The women in these beds had little choice. They could either accept this primitive medical care, or leave themselves and their tiny babies at the mercy of life-threatening diseases. For many, the only choices were to accept poor and limited services, attempt to live with their sickness, or give up and die.

As a former A&E nurse in the UK, I shuddered at the thought of two patients sharing the same bed, and at the hazardous practices that risked spreading infection that I had seen in the last few minutes.

People bustled through the hospital entrance straight into the dim corridor. Large scuff marks were etched into the ageing walls from which paint flaked off in large chunks. A trolley lay abandoned against a wall, discoloured stuffing spilling out from a gash in its middle. This emergency department was full, with beds lining the perimeter of each small room. There was little else in the way of equipment or supplies. Drip stands fed fluids into the despondent forms inhabiting the beds. The atmosphere felt oppressive.

A grimacing man in his thirties was wheeled in on a trolley, forcing another patient to vacate a bed for this new arrival.

The short-stay ICU in the emergency department was differentiated only by a little extra space, a cardiac monitor by each bed, and the greater level of distress evident in the patients: a contorted form in one bed, the heaving chest of a woman struggling for breath in another, and a pained expression on the face of a male patient in another bed. This was a different galaxy from the A&E departments I had worked in as a nurse in the UK.

There were no curtains between the beds, yet a male patient was being cared for in the bed next to the female patients: an unacceptable practice in this culture, where modesty and separation between genders is a prerequisite for treating people with an attitude of respect and decency. Even in the West it would be inconceivable to put a male and female in neighbouring beds without a basic curtain or divider.

We walked to the operating department, which I could see they had made an effort to keep clean, to the best of their ability. But the age and state of disrepair of the equipment, together with the chaotic nature of the environment, with curtains pinned between doorways, would certainly have thwarted some of their best efforts.

Upstairs we were shown the maternity and obstetrics department, where I was welcomed into a room where incubators lined the walls. Miniature sleeping bodies breathed rapidly in each incubator. Their tiny feet were blue with bruises from the blood tests that were part of their care. The cannulas and giving sets for fluids and medications looked enormous taped against their minute hands. I could not imagine leaving a precious baby of mine here, yet there were no mothers or other family members to be seen.

The labour room consisted of three basic birthing beds crammed side by side, with an additional machine for warming and caring for newborn babies. I took a deep breath as I surveyed this room, thinking back to my own birthing experiences in the UK. My first child was born at home with the assistance of two dedicated midwives who came to our house from our local hospital. My second child was born after an induced labour in a hospital room of around the same size as this. But I was the only patient in the room, and I had a team of doctors and midwives, and an anaesthetist who came running when it suddenly became more complicated. When my baby showed signs of distress during my labour and was then born blue, the team sprang into action. While it had been traumatic for my husband and myself, we knew we were in excellent hands. There was every bit of equipment and experience needed to give our youngest child the best chance possible. But if I had given birth here, anything could have happened.

'If they need a caesarean section', I was told, 'they have to go downstairs. There are no operating rooms on this floor.'

As the nurse smiled encouragingly at me, my distressed face gave my feelings away. I began to grapple with what this would mean for any poor woman whose labour took a turn for the worse. My two labours had been unusually quick, but intense and excruciating, and I had no ability to move or walk without a huge amount of encouragement and assistance. Almost as an afterthought, the nurse added that there was no lift.

'Sorry?' I raised my eyebrows. 'No lift?' Surely there must at least be a lift! How else would a woman in distress, experiencing a traumatic or dangerous labour, get downstairs to the operating department I had just walked upstairs from? I could not hide my shock as I asked how a woman would get downstairs for a caesarean if she was already in the middle of giving birth. I felt goosebumps bristling on my arms, and my wide eyes grew still wider as I watched the nurse enact slinging an imaginary woman in labour over her shoulder.

'They have to carry them with their hands,' my translator said in a more conservative manner. I blinked as I stared at her, then back at the nurse again. She was not joking.

'Really?' There was a pleading tone to my voice this time, as I looked from person to person, searching for a sign that perhaps there was another way to move a woman in one of her most painful and vulnerable moments to an operating room on a different floor, at a stage where every second lost could cost the life of her or her baby. Their affirmations that this was the only means of transport now had a more serious air as they registered my dismayed response.

'Wow.' I took a deep breath and looked away. My shock and disbelief were poorly hidden as my mind continued to process what that would mean for a woman in this position. The added risks and discomfort a situation like this would entail for any woman and her baby were hard for me to accept. Aren't these women and their babies worth more than this? Don't their lives matter as much as any of ours in the West? Shouldn't these women, and every patient in this hospital, be able to go through some of their most helpless and agonising moments with dignity and safety too?

The atmosphere in the corridor felt thick and heavy, and I suddenly felt overwhelmed by the accumulation of things I had seen in this hospital that morning. I fought back the d raw emotions bubbling up inside me. I did not want to break down in tears in the middle of this hospital corridor in front of the work associates I had come with, or in front of the staff here who were so stretched.

I swallowed and took many deep breaths, but I could not suppress the feelings. I walked to the outer corridor, where I wiped away the stream of tears. My translator followed me, apologising earnestly for upsetting me. As if any of this was her fault. As if any of this was anyone's fault here. These staff were trying to survive in the middle of a medical crisis induced by eight years of brutal conflict, the deliberate targeting of hospitals, a collapsed economy in which few healthcare professionals earned a living wage, and immoral sanctions imposed against Syria which affect the supply of humanitarian and medical aid. These embargoes choked the life-saving supply system for essential medical equipment, supplies and certain drugs that was so vital to maintaining any kind of effective medical infrastructure. Many medical suppliers outside Syria refuse to supply their products to Syria, regardless of whether they are intended for humanitarian aid for the civilian population, because Syria is under sanctions.

After calming myself, we tried to continue the tour, going next to the renal dialysis unit. A bright and inspiring picture had been hung on the wall of the overfilled room in an attempt to lift the atmosphere. But the melancholy, exhausted faces of the patients packed into that small room, where they were attached to dialysis machines, were too much after everything else. Once more, I had to turn away to hide my brimming tears from the patients who had no choice but to silently accept the limited resources or die, the only two choices available. And these were the lucky ones, as there are others in Syria with renal failure who can't get as many dialysis treatments as they need. We made our way outside to get some fresh air, as I tried to regain some composure while struggling with so many thoughts racing through my mind. I did not want to show any of these precious souls my shock or pity as I looked at their dire situation without being able to change it.

This hospital was on its knees trying to provide for the ordinary and poor people in this city who have little or no ability to pay for healthcare. With only around forty beds, according to the World Health Organisation's definition, this medical centre was now one of the main public hospitals for the entire governorate since the destruction of the main hospital, with its hundreds of beds, that had provided for the poorer people before the war. The medical needs in this city vastly outstripped its available resources. Even in this public hospital, treatment was not guaranteed to be free.

Of the remaining private hospitals, many charged high prices while providing limited or poor care. Many are little more than day-surgery units for simple procedures, with no back-up should complications occur. Many private hospitals in the governorate lack effective teams of specialist doctors, and instead transfer patients to other hospitals, which also lack resources. Some have developed poor reputations for people dying in their care. Many don't admit patients overnight.

Walking around and seeing the weary, resigned faces of the patients, I felt as if my heart had been wrung out. I had seen the epitome of an oversubscribed Third World hospital. I had also seen the desperation and helplessness of the poor. These people were among those who had paid the highest price for eight years of ruthless war in Syria.

Choice is a luxury, and expectation is even more so. We have an abundance of both in the UK, where healthcare is provided free of charge. We have drugs, equipment, disposables, well-trained staff and hospital beds available to us. All of these are assumed and provided. Our National Health Service, by comparison with anything in Syria, is the elite. It is the Ferrari or Lamborghini, or the Four Seasons or Sheraton, of medical provision.

Around a third of the registered hospitals had been destroyed, or else had been damaged and were out of service. The remaining hospitals, public and private, provided far fewer effective inpatient beds than advertised. In the UK, we have thousands of beds to serve the same size population as in this governorate. From working with doctors and suppliers who know each of these hospitals intimately, we know that the reality there is closer to just a few hundred effective and reliable inpatient beds across the entire governorate – for a population of nearly two million! Many of them are in facilities which cannot provide the care they advertise to an international standard. They lack specialist doctors, resources or expertise, or are day-surgery units that close at night.

Currently, if they could, most people would travel outside Syria for medical treatment. Many go to Lebanon rather than use the damaged healthcare system left in the wake of this conflict. We plan to build a not-for-profit hospital working to international standards which gives confidence to the Syrian people that they can receive the care they need without travelling abroad. For many Syrians, the cost of travelling abroad, and of paying for private care in a comparatively expensive place like Lebanon, means that this is not an option.

For each private operation that is paid for in our new hospital, provision will also be made for poor patients who cannot afford to pay. Additionally, there are charities in Syria that receive funding to cover medical assistance to the poor, as well as health insurance companies, but what is lacking are reliable hospitals where treatment can be provided. Everyone needs and deserves quality hospitals, both rich and poor, but through treating the wealthy in our new hospital, we will also be able to offer a high standard of care to the poor too. On this basis, the hospital will be self-sustaining.

Our vision is also to provide a professional, nurturing environment where the next generation of doctors and nurses can train and develop their skills. In the future, we would love to bring doctors and nurses from abroad who can help with training as well as carrying out specialist procedures and treatments, although that would be challenging at the current time.

We trust that God will provide everything needed – the money, the professionals and the materials. We have no choice but to trust him, as we have for every aspect of this work to date. There is no question that we need to work hard, as well as to make and implement careful and responsible plans to make this happen, as we have with every project we have run to date. But ultimately, he is our strength, ability, wisdom and provision.

22

Love the Jihadists

Access to this high-security area in Ghouta was restricted. Our identity documents were inspected at the first checkpoint marking the entrance to this controlled zone. The contrast between the busy road we had just left, with much still intact, and the empty one on which we were now travelling, with much damage, was stark.

This road had been inaccessible to the general public from outside the area since the early part of the conflict, when it had first been taken by armed militants. Although they could hardly believe what was happening, people across the country quickly learnt of the events taking place inside the areas in and around east Ghouta. They heard from the people who fled, as well as from the people who stayed behind, but communications soon became more difficult from inside these areas. Many saw the horror with their own eyes, and many lost family members when they were killed by the groups who took these areas. Some of these places remained under siege for five or six years.

One of our team had told me of his own experiences during the early part of the conflict. He described how he was intimidated out of a café on the border of eastern Ghouta. He had visited this café for years, but one day the owners and other customers behaved in a very hostile way towards him. They made it clear that, as a Christian, he was now unwelcome there. That day a radical Muslim cleric was being broadcast on the TV in that café, and he was speaking against the 'infidels' who didn't support their ideology and giving instructions on how they should be treated. This included Christians, Shia Muslims, Druze and other minority groups. The message to this man was crystal clear, and he left immediately. A week later, a Christian friend of his was threatened in the same café and chased to his car. It wasn't long before eastern Ghouta and some surrounding areas were under siege.

The dusty road we were now driving along was deserted. With barely a soul in sight, this district was an abandoned remnant of a different reality. Ragged, gaping holes now replaced windows and doors. The spaces where walls had once been were framed by tattered brickwork in the sparse buildings distributed along the roadside. All were damaged or decaying. Yet despite the dearth of people travelling this road, there were still checkpoints to pass through.

Fading paint depicted the unmistakable black, white and green of the Free Syrian Army flag still evident on some of the walls by the road. In this area recently taken back to government control, even the oil drums which marked every checkpoint in Syria still displayed the Free Syrian Army colours rather than the red, white and black seen at every checkpoint in government-controlled areas.

On our arrival at this, one of the centres for displaced people with the highest security, our entry was stopped. Our cars sat in front of the closed, unforgiving iron gate while soldiers asked questions. They did not appear to be shifting. Time dragged on as we waited.

The amount of waiting involved when doing anything in Syria is something my impatient nature has had to adjust to over recent years, as nothing happens quickly in this country. A foreigner linked to humanitarian work is under great scrutiny. And any suspicions are multiplied exponentially for a citizen from a country such as Britain, which is linked with the hostilities in Syria. So many have lost their faith in love and humanity after so many years of fighting and hate, coupled with endless deception and lies. Too often, humanitarian work has been used by external governments and intelligence agencies as a cover under which to accomplish aims which serve political interests, rather than simply serving the ordinary people.

The soldiers checked our ID documents and continued with their calls. These high levels of security were unsurprising. As

well as the civilian families who fled eastern Ghouta as the siege
was being broken, this high-security accommodation centre for
the displaced also housed some of the jihadist fighters who had
killed, maimed and tortured so many during their reign. Before
the heaviest and most intense bombing campaigns to break the
siege, it was reported that leaflets had been airdropped over the
area. These leaflets gave the fighters and civilians three options:
to stay and face the heavy, brutal bombardment aimed at returning
the area to government control; to leave through the humanitarian corridors which had been opened for people to escape
the besieged area for the first time in five years; or, for those
unwilling to accept the administration of the Syrian government,
to be evacuated out on buses which mostly went to Idlib.

This centre was now hosting just a small proportion of the
masses who had fled through the humanitarian corridors earlier
in the year. Men, women, children, the elderly, the young, those
injured or unwell, and also some of the jihadists and their families had been received here.

After many years of fighting and violence, many of the men
involved in the combat were now tired and disillusioned. Many
saw what the years of fighting and control under these groups
had created in this area, which was far worse than the existence
they had lived before in Syria. They were weary and had chosen
to lay down their weapons.

Their motivations for fighting had been varied. Some had
supported the ideology of establishing a state governed by Islamic
rule, while others had been poor and simple men in desperate
need of money to survive. The groups who took control of
these areas were supported by wealthy entities outside Syria, and
had offered a better chance – or perhaps the only chance – of
an income for many residents of these areas once they were
under their control. After the sieges began, survival had become
increasingly difficult. Many people had been coerced, pressured,
or forced into joining the groups of fighters, or simply swept
along by the events taking place around them. There have been
many accounts of those who refused, and their families, having
been physically abused, humiliated, imprisoned, or killed.

I have often wondered how we would have dealt with a similar scenario unfolding around us in the UK. What if Croydon, on the outskirts of London, was suddenly taken over by an armed group, recruiting the men in the area and restricting people's movements? If we were hungry and unable to feed our children, and were fearful of the controlling group, how many of us would be strong enough to stand against the evil around us?

Leaving the area was impossible for most, with many reports of individuals who tried to escape being killed by the controlling armed groups, for whom the ordinary and the vulnerable had enormous value as human shields. As a result, fear was, no doubt, at the heart of some of the decisions made by the men who fought alongside the jihadists. What would happen to them or their families if they refused? There was no escaping, so they had to try to survive in their besieged area.

Finally, a soldier began to push back the large iron double gates. Another soldier collected our identity documents while instructing us that taking any photographs inside was forbidden. I felt vulnerable leaving my passport with the soldiers at the gate, but there was no negotiation to be done here. These were their conditions for entry: we could take them or leave them.

As our car rolled into the inhabited part of the camp, a surreal sight lay before us. Men in every attitude and pose were scattered everywhere. I could only see men. I hadn't been sure what to expect in visiting this centre now. Since the distributions of clothes and essential aid our team had done there with partners in late spring and early summer, a significant percentage of the displaced families who had been there at that time had now returned to their homes (if they had not been destroyed). But those left behind were either those who had nothing to return to, or the people who were viewed as being more dangerous.

Men in their twenties to fifties were scattered all around this camp. Some were occupied with daily tasks like washing at the outdoor sinks erected at large red water tanks. Others sat on walls in small groups, looking bored, with nothing to do, just passing the time, which must have seemed endless in such a

place. Two makeshift kiosk stalls had been put up, where essential supplies could be bought by those who were able to find a
source of money. Most of the remaining men here now were
the fighters who had given up their weapons. They, too, had
now been reduced to nothing. They had left everything behind,
and were living in UN tents lined up in the muddy grounds of
this walled centre.

As we pulled up by the main building, the men stopped what
they were doing to watch us. Those washing turned to gaze. Those
on the other side of the water tanks craned their necks to get a
better view, while those who were sitting now stood in order to
see this curious vision. Never had I felt as conspicuous as I did
while we got out of the car and walked into the main building.

A sea of eyes followed us, and I smiled warmly at each of
the men we passed, trying not to stare back at them. I was just
as curious to study and understand who they were, as they were
to know who we were. The two women I saw while I was
there were covered in traditional long Islamic clothing and hijabs.
Two long-haired females – one with blue eyes and an obviously
western appearance – in our group otherwise comprised of men
made an unusual spectacle in this isolated and restricted centre.
Visitors were few here, especially uncovered females.

The building was unkempt, with the characteristic old blankets hung in all the doorways leading off to individual rooms.
Yet with rubbish and dirt lining the corridors, this looked more
unloved than any other communal shelters I had visited in Syria
over the last few years. Perhaps the unbalanced ratio of male to
female residents was the defining factor, or perhaps it was the
chaotic lives these people had lived for years in a besieged area.

We were led behind a grey blanket hanging in a doorway
into the one-room living area of one of the few remaining
families there. Leaving our shoes at the entrance, we took our
seats on the thin mats lining the walls of the room. This was
one of the families which had fled east Ghouta as the siege was
being broken. They, along with the other newly displaced people
who came to this centre, had received some of the clothes, shoes
and hygiene items we had sent in the aid that was distributed

in this centre around six months earlier. This had been part of the much larger distributions of aid we had sent from the UK across Ghouta to more than a hundred thousand people.

It was clear from what this woman and her husband didn't say, as well as from what they did say, that they had been linked to the succession of jihadist groups which had controlled their village during the siege. They did not have the deprived appearance of others I had met who had lived under siege. On the contrary, this woman and some of her children were very overweight, and clearly had not experienced the effects of food deprivation which others living in the area had talked of. Her demeanour was very different to that of the women I had sat with who had wept uncontrollably, with pain written on their faces, as they told me their gut-wrenching stories.

After a number of years of working daily with people on the ground in Syria, visiting the country a number of times, and meeting with a multitude of families displaced from many key areas in the conflict, I had learnt to read between the lines of what I saw and what I was told. There is an enormous amount to be missed from listening only to the surface story without understanding the context.

With the 3D magic eye pictures so popular in the 1990s, which at first sight appeared to be no more than a hash of colours, tiny shapes and patterns, most people were unable to see the picture which lay behind the strange arrangement of shapes. It was only after understanding and, with practice, after fixing your eyes in a certain way that the image would suddenly appear, in 3D, with crystal-clear definition. In the same way, listening to the stories of the people and hearing what they didn't say as much as what they did say, and how they said it, as well as taking into account their demeanors their choice of words, their descriptions, their experiences, and also how these differed from the experiences of others living in the same besieged areas, gave clarity to the situation. Fear of, or allegiances to, the groups controlling each area filtered the accounts people gave.

The woman said she had done unskilled manual work, and

that her husband had done labouring work where they lived before the war. Life had been hard, she said, but they had managed to feed their children. When the war started in this area, she said it became a big struggle even just to find bread to eat, and they were reduced to begging. Once their neighbourhood in eastern Ghouta came under siege, it had swapped from the control of one armed group to that of another. Most undisputedly espoused extremist ideologies and practices.

When I asked about schooling, she said that none of her children had learnt to read or write in eastern Ghouta, although most were school age. As she talked, the youngest of her nine children drifted off to sleep in her arms. I asked what effect the experience of living under siege had had on her children. None, she had assured us, saying they were all 100% normal. I was surprised to hear this. They, like most of the Syrian children I have met across the country, sat silently beside their mother while she talked.

She said her husband had not worked during the years eastern Ghouta had been under siege. But her weight, and that of her children, depicted a family who had had an excess of food over recent years. Somehow, they had received an income and/or a good supply of food from doing some kind of work or service during this time, while others reported having gone hungry. They clearly didn't wish to disclose anything about their income and it was not my place to ask.

As we talked, the personality of her husband came through. He was confident and authoritative, and ordered his daughters around in a domineering way. With all the elements of their circumstances and story, I was left in little doubt as to this family's connections with the jihadist groups that controlled the area they came from. The situation was extremely sensitive, and there were things I could ask and things I couldn't, or wouldn't, out of sensitivity. And there were things they could say, and things they couldn't or wouldn't.

I wondered what part this man might have played in the events which took place there. Had he been one of the organisers, or had he been one of the men who fired rockets or shells?

Was he one of the men who had beheaded or shot the people who didn't comply with the rules, or had he looked on as others carried out the punishments? His toned, muscular body suggested that he had been physically active. What had been his motivation for joining the militants? Was it desperation simply to earn an income so that his family could eat, or were his motivations ideological? If his wife's earlier comments were indicative, they had struggled to feed their children and had probably found themselves in a desperate situation characterised by neglect. What other choice was there but to join the fighters if they couldn't escape?

Steering clear of the sensitive issues, I asked about their hopes for the future. The mother told us she wanted to return to her village in east Ghouta, to start life again and watch her children grow up. She told us how she had been able to go back and visit their home, but had found nothing left. She had thought about taking a tent and putting it in the place where her house had stood, and living in it with her family while trying to rebuild their home, stone by stone. What a pitifully sad picture, and what woeful aspiration for the future.

If this family had been part of the fighting in eastern Ghouta, however bloody this may have been, and however right or wrong they had been, they were also the victims of it. They, too, had lost everything. The future was as uncertain for them as it was for any civilian. What had these poor and simple people been converted into over these last years? The choices they had been forced to make were beyond imagination for any westerner who has grown up in a safe environment with law and order, the existence of a welfare state, a free healthcare service and a comparatively comfortable life.

As we left, I hugged and kissed this woman and her children, wondering what sense they would make of the circumstances they had lived so far, and of the impact this may have on their lives and ideologies in the future. I felt compassion for this woman and her children. Clearly there were things she was saying that were untrue, but could anyone blame her? It stirred up my compassion, and an overwhelming sense of the injustice of war, for everyone involved, on every side. The poorest, least educated are the ones who are most easily manipulated and recruited to fight by the drivers of conflict. For many in the West, the boundaries between right and wrong seem so black and white, but in a place like eastern Ghouta and many other parts of Syria which fell under siege, when put to the test, those boundaries became extremely grey and muddied for many. What would each of us have done if faced with the same situation, and with a need to survive and feed our own children?

The price paid in this conflict has been exorbitantly high; around half a million people were killed, and one and a half million were left physically disabled. That is the legacy of this generation. Immense damage has been caused to the infrastructure, and to the very fabric and culture of this country. There are diametrically opposed opinions about the political situation in Syria, but who, on any side of this war, could say even for a moment that this conflict has brought anything positive to this nation? This war has brought only devastation, destruction, loss and suffering.

Before the war there were certainly problems in Syria, and some were very serious. But despite this, every Syrian child could access a free education. There was also basic free healthcare provision for those who couldn't afford, or didn't want to pay for, private care. There were universities, and medical schools linked to acceptable hospitals where doctors could train, and there was a strong sense of community. Yet so many of these good things in Syria have now been damaged or destroyed, without changing or improving any of the things that were an issue or needed changing before the war.

Syria has been set back decades through what has been lost during this war, not just in the infrastructure of the country, but also in the community. People have seen such savagery and betrayal. Many lost their humanity; ordinary law-abiding citizens became rapists, murderers, extortionists and thieves Many lost their trust in each other, in their communities, and too many Syrian people have been lost to other countries. These people are needed to rebuild the country. There have been no winners in this war. No one has gained, yet everyone has lost something or someone. Many have lost everything. Whoever was fighting, on each side, and whatever their reason, everyone has suffered in some way. Everyone. Without exception.

This cruel war has also cost the hearts and souls of the men on every side who have been instrumental in fighting. They will live with the cries of the people they have killed echoing in their ears, with the images in their minds of men, women and children as they died. They live now with blood on their hands, as whatever their reason for killing, taking a life from a fellow human being has consequences for each human soul.

Many of these men who joined the extremists had wives and children. The burning question is what will happen to them? Huge numbers of men, who fought with the jihadists, together with their families, are still alive. What will these men be now, and what will become of their children? These men have to try to make a fresh start, and to begin living civilian lives again. Somehow, they must begin the process of reconciliation with their neighbours, their nation, but also with themselves. How will they live, side by side, with the people they traumatised, humiliated and physically abused for years? Can they ever be accepted again?

It will take enormous courage, humility and forgiveness for all affected, the abusers and the abused, to try to start again. For the abusers have not just hurt others, but in every atrocity they have committed, they have also damaged a part of themselves. In torturing and abusing a mother, father or child, they have damaged their own humanity as well. In humiliating and reducing someone else to a nothing and a nobody, they have allowed evil to fester and grow in their own hearts. The blood they have on their hands is not easy to wipe off. It sticks to their fingers and leaves stains which can only be removed by a miracle of unconditional love, forgiveness and reunion. How else can these fellow human beings have any hope of a fresh start, and of a future that is not simply a distorted development of a violent and bloody past?

Our approach to humanity in this work has been to hold

out an olive branch to anyone in need, to demonstrate unconditional love, forgiveness and non-judgemental acceptance. These men have laid down their guns, their positions and their pride, and in the process, they have lost everything too. Now, as they start over again with nothing, many of them with families to support, what can anyone hope for, for the children of the jihadist fighters?

Does a five-year-old girl deserve to be punished for the mistakes of her father? Can any child choose the family into which they are born? Should they be forced to pay the price for their parents' choices any more than they already have or will? No. They are children. They didn't kill anyone. These children are the future generation of Syria, and they need to be loved and nurtured if the community in Syria is to be rebuilt.

Can anything change the heart of an extremist who has been driven for years by desperation, fear, extremism and hate? Judgement and social exclusion will not. They will simply exacerbate an already raw and painful wound. The only things which have greater power than these negative responses, which are more instinctive for many, are love, compassion, mercy and grace. All of these are qualities and blessings that God poured out for all of us through Jesus.

It is a mistake to think any of us are better than these jihadist armies, or than any of the political figures, governments and entities that have been party to this conflict. Each of us could have ended up in the same position as each of them, had we been born in a different place, to a different family, being taught a different set of values and ideologies, or had we been faced with the same kind of struggles to feed our families. But the blessings each of us have had, if we have had the opportunity to live a different life and learn a different set of attitudes, give us a greater burden of responsibility to reach out to those who have been sold the lies and deception that brought them to this humbled, rocky place. When we reach out in love to these people, we reconcile ourselves, too, with what we might have become if we had walked in their shoes.

Jesus' instructions to us were so clear. Forgive those who hurt you, pray for and love your enemies. Give to everyone who asks, care for those who are sick, feed those who are hungry, clothe those who are naked, and visit those who are in prison. His message is one of mercy and grace. His teaching is an instruction in unconditional love. Only through undeserved love can the wounds of humanity, and the devastation we have caused, be healed.

23

Rebuilding the Ruins

The Return to the Vision for Grace,
December 2018 to January 2019

One evening, Dr A told me that one of our connections had offered him a partnership in establishing a medical centre in a safe and highly functioning area of one of the cities in Syria. An NGO we had worked with was in the process of building a medical centre, but had not established who would equip, staff or run it. The organisation wanted to establish a private medical centre to support an orphanage and other disadvantaged groups.

As we talked, I felt increasingly excited about the idea, until I heard that 'still, small voice of calm' once again telling me not to be unequally yoked to unbelievers. Again, I struggled. I had a huge amount of respect for the founder of this NGO, who, over the years, had done so much wonderful work.

But we had learnt our lesson earlier in the year about taking counsel from the Lord, so Dr A and I agreed we should pray before going any further. The next morning, I asked God for guidance as to whether we should take on this medical centre, then opened the Bible randomly. It opened at Ezra 8, which detailed how Ezra gathered people together to return to Jerusalem. They camped on the bank of the river Ahava, then fasted and prayed for protection on their journey.

Although I had asked about this new medical project, I felt God had directed me back to focus on the big project for Grace (Jerusalem) Hospital, and for which he had given us a vision eighteen months earlier. It had been chugging along in the background, but it had taken these eighteen months for us to gain the final planning sign-offs for a 9,000-square-metre hospital. I had met with an architect a few weeks before while I was in

Syria, but progress was slow as our other pressing projects usually ended up taking priority. I realised now that if we took on this new medical centre, although it would be providing a much-needed service, it would also be a significant distraction from our big hospital. We felt that this was an instruction not to be diverted from our mission.

We were aware we needed to be very careful not to assume that every passage we found in the Bible relating to Jerusalem or the Temple was linked to our hospital, as so much of the Bible talks of these! But I believe God, in these specific situations, gave us the discernment to know what he wanted us to understand from him. It has been essential for us to prayerfully weigh every passage before using them as we have – though I should point out that this is not the only way we make decisions.

I don't get an answer every time I ask for guidance then open the Bible randomly. This has been especially so when I have asked him a second time to guide me on something he has already answered in the past. There have been a number of occasions when, wanting reassurance, I have gone back to ask him to guide me in something that he has already given me an answer to. He has not answered the same question twice. I felt in these instances that he was demonstrating that he doesn't change, and his answers haven't changed. His Word remains the same, yesterday, today and tomorrow. We need to trust the answer he gives us.

As I read the passage, I also felt a stirring in my heart when I read how the people fasted and prayed. They had a long and potentially dangerous journey ahead of them. So they camped for three days on the riverbank, summoned ministers from the Temple of God, and proclaimed a fast to humble themselves before God and pray for wise guidance for their journey, their people and their possessions. They were embarrassed to ask the earthly king for protection, so they asked God. I felt very strongly it would be sensible for us, too, to take some time out to fast and pray for protection and guidance as we began this huge journey to design and build a new hospital. The architect I had met in Syria estimated the cost for our new hospital would be in the region of $20 million, which was a huge amount. I sent the passage from Ezra to Dr A, who immediately spotted the subtitle 'Return to Jerusalem' and agreed to fast and pray with me for three days. Another member of our prayer group fasted the three days with us, and others joined us for one of the three days.

I woke during the first night of fasting, having had strange dreams. The first was about travelling along a road, then being in a house with some familiar people. We then saw that the house was surrounded by snakes, which we went out and killed, one by one, piling them up on a plate. We then started talking about cooking them to eat. There was one snake that it took three blows with a knife to sever its head. The second dream was about travelling in a car, then being stopped and forced to get out by the Syrian authorities to answer a lot of questions. At first they were very suspicious of me, but after asking lots of questions they relaxed towards me after seeing that I was like family to members of our team, and everything was OK.

The next day, we spent time praying and reading though the passages in Ezra again. In the afternoon, Dr A received an unexpected phone call. It was a government employee who was involved in gaining the authorisations needed for importing and distributing our containers. He said we should stop bringing in containers to distribute for now. There was no acceptable official explanation. What did this mean? Was it linked to one of my dreams? I had no choice but to cancel the next aid appeal.

On the third day of fasting, we spent time praying and seeking God's will about the future of the field hospital in Deir ez-Zor, and about whether we should continue running this or put our efforts completely into the big hospital. We opened our Bibles at random. Dr A opened at Haggai.

The first passage he looked at was subtitled 'Obedience to God's Call'. This passage and the verses leading up to it were about God's instruction and promise to the people who, after much delay, would finally rebuild the Temple in Jerusalem: 'Why are you living in luxurious houses while my house lies in ruins?' (Haggai 1:4 NLT). He instructed them to start work rebuilding the Temple. For the second time that week, we had asked God for guidance about a different project, and both times the passages we were led to were about Jerusalem.

As we read through Haggai, every part was related to the issue of rebuilding the Temple and hence could be connected with our project of building this hospital. More importantly, in it God gave a promise about the blessings to come once the work was fully under way.

Lately, each of the projects we had on the ground in Syria had been exceptionally time consuming. The pressing and urgent issues which came up in appeals, in distributions and in our small but very high-maintenance field hospital needed immediate responses. But we felt now that God was showing us that, at least at this stage, he wanted us to focus on the planning, designing and building, and fundraising for this new hospital. We now had no excuse for not making it our number one priority.

The situation in Syria had changed so much in the last two years. It was important we adapted our approach to ensure that our focus remained on meeting the needs for the future, rather than simply continuing in the same attitude of emergency response as we had had two or three years before, during the height of the fighting, when hundreds of thousands were being continually displaced. Patching people up in small field hospitals was not enough on its own now. They needed specialist services that can't be provided in these small and basic settings. Significant rebuilding of the essential life-saving infrastructure was needed to stop people dying from conditions that can so easily be treated. It was not just about repairing what had been destroyed, it was about rebuilding something new, something more inspiring, to serve the people's most basic needs, but in the most meaningful way. Syria is in need of transformation, and the people them-selves, as well as each community, need restoration, new life and new hope.

We chose the name 'Grace' for this hospital. Our vision is for this hospital to be unlike the other hospitals in Syria. It will be a not-for-profit Christian hospital which exists to make high quality medical care available for all, affordable and accessible to the poor. We want a visible, tangible and fresh demonstration of God's grace and blessings for the Syrian people who have remained in, and who are returning to, their home country.

We want it to exceed the expectations of such a hospital in Syria. Our vision is for it to be advanced and appealing. It is ideally situated to serve some of the neediest people. It will be innovative in its approach to medical care. Clinical areas will be designed to ensure logical adjacencies, ease of cleaning and minimal spread of infections, but this hospital will also be a welcoming refuge for people in the most vulnerable times of their lives.

We want to invest in the people and equipment that enable us to provide an environment where Syrian medical professionals can train and develop their skills and expertise. We hope one day to be able to send expert medical teams from outside Syria to help train the doctors and nurses in Syria and develop their skills, although this would be challenging for many reasons as things currently stand. Medical expertise in specialist areas is at a low in Syria, and we are keen to play a part in raising standards and expectations in both medical and nursing care.

It may be not for profit, but it shouldn't look like a Third World hospital. We want to create an environment which gives an atmosphere of light and hope. All decor throughout the hospital should reflect Jesus' message of love: 'I am the light of the world. Whoever follows me will never walk in darkness, but will have the light of life' (John 8:12).

Our vision is for the hospital's chapel to be a hub, a place where people can gather to worship God and pray for one another. Our desire is that this chapel will serve as an outreach centre for the most at-risk patients, looking beyond their medical conditions. We want to give pastoral care to patients and their families, in particular reaching out to the neediest, who may need ongoing support or encouragement.

It will be our privilege to host and serve people in need from every community in Syria, regardless of their faith, political views or anything else which may make them different. Emphasis on these differences has been used to break down the Syrian community during these years of conflict, and we want to hold out an olive branch to everyone, demonstrating love and acceptance at the heart of our work. The love and presence of our living God; Father, Son and Holy Spirit, will be the glory inside this hospital.

At the beginning of January, Dr A's father had a vision. He had been asking God if this hospital would really happen. In this vision, Jesus confirmed to him that the hospital would be built, that he would be inside it, and that it would be his house. This was very beautiful, confirming and encouraging for all of us. I also felt that I personally needed some direct encouragement from God too. A week or so later I had been praying intensely, asking God to give me a sign that we were progressing in the right direction for his vision. I was very focused, working hard, yet this was a bigger project than anything I had done before. I wanted more reassurance.

About a week later, at church, I went forward for prayer at the end of the service. Without me saying anything, a woman put her hand on my shoulder and began to pray. She was new to the church and I had never seen her before. I didn't know her name, and she didn't know anything about me or my work. I didn't say anything to her, as God knows my heart. She just prayed freely.

After praying for a few minutes, she had a prophetic picture of a pomegranate, and told me that the many seeds in it represented a harvest that would come from me. She talked about how difficult it is to get through the tough layer of skin to reach the many seeds of fruit inside. I was very moved. When I had been in Syria a couple of months before, Dr A and his wife had saved some of the end-of-season pomegranates on the trees for me to pick. One morning, we had gone into the garden and I picked some. He had cut them open with a knife before handing them to me to eat. They are one of my favourite fruits, and Syrian pomegranates are the best I have ever tasted. After picking them, we spent some time praying for God's anointing of Dr A, and he even took a photo of me sitting under a pomegranate tree holding one of the fruits that he had cut open. I don't know why, it just seemed like a good idea at the time. It wasn't something I had discussed with anyone here in England afterwards as there hadn't been any reason to.

Encouraged, I spoke to the lady who had been praying, telling her that my work was in Syria, where I had been picking pomegranates just a couple of months before. I told her that her prophetic picture was really special, particularly as God had given us a vision to design and build a Christian hospital in Syria which was bigger than anything we had done before. I only said a few words to her, not enough for her to be able to include such detail in her words which followed. This convinced me that these words came straight from God.

She began to prophesy in the name of Jesus, saying many things whose significance she couldn't have understood. I still had not told our supporters how God had used the passages in the Bible about the rebuilding of the Temple in Jerusalem to speak to us about building our hospital. I certainly hadn't mentioned this in the couple of sentences I had said to this lady. I asked her to repeat some of what she had said so that I could remember it, so she suggested I recorded it on my phone, which I did.

She said she felt the Lord saying this hospital would be a house of refuge, that it would be built solidly and securely, that it carries legacy and longevity. She said the Lord was saying it would not be stopped, either by government agencies or by bombs, and that the allocated place for it will be safe. She said there is supernatural protection over the establishment of this, and over me personally, as well as over the physical building itself. She said she felt the Lord was saying to me there are very specific timings for the pursuit of this project, and he is at work behind the scenes. When it gets to places when it feels like things have stopped, we are not to panic, but instead he wants us to use those times to rest and be restored, and for the team to come together.

She said she felt the Lord saying he is bringing a special team of gifted people to this project, that she saw legal people, those who can translate, and those who have all the skills we need. She said, 'God is saying it is like the building of the Temple, where the Lord anointed very special craftsmen, very specific people, to come and establish something that has longevity.' As soon as she said 'building the Temple', I couldn't stop my tears flowing through everything else she said after that.

She said the Lord says he has some very clear completion timings for each stage of the project, that he wants me to know that he is with me, and that he is going to release gifts of faith. She said she saw three very specific gifts of faith, for impossible things. She said that God would promise things which I would accept in faith, and would hold in my heart, as Mary held the promise God gave her in her heart, saying 'let it be' (Luke 1:38 ESV).

She said, 'The Lord says you are not carrying this alone, he is bringing in help. He is bringing in those who have an equal strength, an equal anointing, and equal vision.' She said that when I build my team, this is what the Lord wants me to look for: people who are my equal in their ability to carry things in faith, in their skill set, in their character. That I won't feel like I am the one dragging everyone along with me. Instead, God is giving his most amazing grace, and this would be lifted and carried.

She finished by saying that the Lord says, 'Please know that your personal restoration is in this restoration. I see you. I don't just see the work. You are my beloved and precious child. I know your needs. I know your heart cries. These cries are not just for the work. I am bringing what you need, even to you. You will be blessed.'

This message came directly from God, through her. Everything she said was as if she had been walking with me through this whole journey, knowing my heart intimately, yet I had never met her before, and she knew nothing about our work. But God knows, and had walked with us through every step of the journey. He spoke to me through her that day, and it was such a moving and humbling experience. It was a deeply personal message, and no one except someone who knew me, my faith and my journey intimately could have said these things. My heavenly Father knows me more deeply and personally than anyone in this world. He graciously gave me this powerful message of encouragement, this signpost, just as I had asked him to.

These were such important assurances. I believe God wanted to prepare and encourage me, as less than two weeks later I suddenly found myself facing a campaign of vicious attacks from some individuals in Syria opposed to our work who were trying to discredit me and my work, and undermine my integrity and honesty. I held tightly to these promises which helped me weather the storms that were fast approaching.

This is how our loving Father works. He is kind, gentle and encouraging. He pushes us beyond our abilities, to help us grow, and disciplines us if we veer off course. When we seek him he gives us everything we need. But when he pushes us to our limits, he walks with us while we are being stretched. It was such a beautiful encounter.

Over those weeks before, the team for this project had been on my mind as I was aware we needed more people both in the UK and in Syria, new people, bringing energy and capability but also the ability to work in the same Spirit-led, prophetic way we had been working over the last few years. It truly is a unique skill set.

24

The Spiritual War

On the Christmas Eve before the prophecy, I had an unusual warning. A couple of months before, a friend had suggested I read Nehemiah, feeling there were many similarities between our vision to design and build a hospital in Syria and the way many families had taken responsibility for rebuilding parts of the wall around Jerusalem. It was certainly an enormous team effort. That night before Christmas, having not yet taken the chance to read it, I sat in the quietness by the glowing fire, after my family had gone to bed, feeling suddenly compelled to read it.

I was very stirred when I read chapter four, detailing the opposition Nehemiah faced in his work rebuilding the wall, and my skin began to bristle with goosebumps. I felt as if God was speaking directly to me through these passages. It talked about how Sanballat and Tobiah, from beyond the Great River, were furious about the wall being rebuilt, and they plotted to come together, to fight against Jerusalem and to cause confusion. At this time God's people prayed and brought in support, stationing armed guards in the places where there were gaps where the wall had not yet been rebuilt. It described how half the people worked, while half remained on guard, and it detailed how those who worked on rebuilding the wall did so working with one hand, while holding a weapon in the other. They were on high alert at all times.

I underlined many of the verses in that chapter, with a strong feeling that the Holy Spirit was showing me the importance of us, too, working with our 'weapons in our hands'. But our weapons are spiritual, not physical, as the battles we face are 'not against flesh and blood, but against the rulers, against the authorities, against the powers of this dark world and against the spiritual forces of evil in the heavenly realms' (Eph. 6:12). I felt very strongly that our 'weapons' are prayer and worship to God the father, Son and Holy Spirit in this spiritual war. As I had seen so clearly a couple of years before when we had to evacuate our first field Hospital, worship is an extremely powerful form of defence against the enemies of God. I photographed this passage in chapter four with the verses I had underlined and sent them to our team in Syria, saying I felt God wanted us to give more priority to the time we spend in prayer and worship in the coming year.

As I read on to chapter six, I felt a very intense and over-whelming feeling, that I can only describe as being like a sixth sense, as I read about the conspiracy against Nehemiah. I felt so strongly that I was being given a specific warning about an attack that we would face in the future. I underlined more verses from chapter six, which I felt were significant. It said that when Sanballat, Tobiah, Geshem the Arab and the rest of the enemies of God's people heard that Nehemiah had rebuilt the wall, Sanballat and Geshem sent a message asking him to meet with them. But Nehemiah knew they were planning to harm him, so refused to meet them.

They sent four messages like this and then, the fifth time, Sanballat sent a letter saying people were reporting that Nehemiah and his people were planning a rebellion against the king. They threatened that these reports would reach the king, urging Nehemiah to take counsel with them. Knowing that they wanted to harm him, and were hoping to try to frighten and weaken them, Nehemiah replied saying they were making it up from their imaginations, and that these accusations were untrue. He prayed, asking God to strengthen his hands. After Nehemiah saw through a further attempt from them to stop him from working, he then continued receiving letters from Tobiah who was trying to scare him.

I read and underlined these passages, feeling a conviction that God was warning us about a coming attack, which might take the form of some kind of false accusations. I was keen to warn our people in Syria, so I photographed these passages too and sent them over, saying what was on my mind. I urged them to read through this book of the Bible, and especially these passages a few times, to be prepared for whatever was coming, and also to be sure that we dedicated more time to prayer and worshipping God. We read the book and reread some of the chapters and passages a few times. Over the next couple of nights, I was drawn back to those passages. But after a few days I forgot about them.

I had assumed that I was being warned about accusations that would be made towards our team in Syria. I also assumed that this was something that would happen further in the future, maybe a year or two down the line, when we were physically building something.

A few weeks later in January, I received the very encouraging prophecy at church with the prophetic picture of the pomegranate and the words about 'building the temple'. In the last few years I have observed that God gives very in-depth and specific prophecies and pictures, or visions, as a means of encouragement, in advance of or during difficult times. He is so faithful and shows us so much mercy. In retrospect, I looked back and felt that this prophecy was an example of this.

Six weeks after Christmas, and two weeks after this prophecy, I suddenly found myself under attack by some people working together, making false accusations against me. One of them sent me many bizarre accusations, the most strange and overarching being that my goal was 'to bring down the Syrian Government', and trying to intimidate and pressure me to meet with their contacts in Syria. Another person began sending me messages through social media pressuring me to engage with him and link him with our representative in Syria, so he could meet our contacts. Their connections began writing and circulating false allegations against me.

A few days after this started, one of our faithful prayer warriors sent a message to our prayer group saying that while she was praying for me, our team and our work, she felt God had put the conspiracy against Nehemiah, in chapter six, on her heart for me. When I saw this message, I was astonished. In the busy-ness of the last weeks, and in spite of the similarities of the events over the preceding few days, I had forgotten all about this passage, its significance, and the way I had felt so intensely that God used it to warm me about a coming attack. As I reread the passage, I was stunned by the similarities between the account in the Bible and the situation I was facing. While on first glance these attacks against me could be seen to be a big misunderstanding on their part, I quickly had a sense that it wasn't as simple as that. After I was reminded of the passages in Nehemiah 6, I felt that, as well as being a warning for me, it was also an instruction in how to deal with the situation. I sensed I was being warned not to engage with or meet with any of these individuals, which was reiterated by our lawyers, and also to go to every length to protect the team working with us on the ground in Syria.

The following week, when talking with one of our trustees, she recounted to me how she had asked her vicar to pray for this situation. His immediate response, without knowing any of these other details of our words about Nehemiah, was to say 'The devil doesn't have any new tricks. Just look at Nehemiah.' When I heard this I was really amazed, and felt sure that this was a threefold, prophetic confirmation from God, to leave me in no doubt that he was walking beside me, guiding me, every step of the way in this difficult part of the journey.

Although it was so hard and hurtful to be falsely accused in such a public way, I also felt so encouraged to know that God is so loving and kind to first warn, then encourage, and then to confirm his reassurance through the difficult times. Over those weeks he walked so closely with me and I felt his presence.

A couple of months later I was speaking at a women's break-fast. One of the women told me she had heard me speak the year before, and had been trying to talk with me afterwards, but she couldn't as there were others waiting to talk with me, so she eventually went home. She explained that she had wanted to talk with me to tell me that throughout my talk, she could see a 'glow' around me. She said that when others got up on the stage she couldn't see it around them, and when I moved from one place to another it stayed with me. When she asked God what it meant, he said it means, 'I've got her back' as in, he is looking out for and defending me. She asked if it meant anything to me.

I was very moved and thanked her, saying yes, it meant a lot to me, and I was grateful for her sharing this. After a few minutes, I thought out loud as I was talking to her, that God's timing is truly remarkable. If she had had the opportunity to talk to me the day she had this experience, I probably would have thanked her and felt perhaps a little bemused, then forgotten about it as there wasn't anything for me to apply it to. I am blessed with a community of beautiful and faithful believers around me, who often share encouraging and prophetic words, but I don't remember many of them unless they have a specific meaning in the situations I am facing. God knows this, and I felt that he therefore gave her the opportunity to tell me at a different time, when its meaning would be very clear and significant. When I explained why it was very important, she too was amazed.

It was reassuring to remember that many of God's messengers in the Bible, and even Jesus himself, were lied about and falsely accused. Jesus was accused of driving out demons by the power of the devil, and the religious leaders at the time found people who were prepared to give false testimony about him in court. Many of the prophets of the Old Testament – Jeremiah, King David, and Joseph, to name a few – were falsely accused, some were imprisoned as a result, and others were persecuted, even to death. John the Baptist was put in prison unjustly; Jesus' disciples and those who followed faced false accusations and persecution.

Jesus warned us that the servant is not above the master, and that we should expect the same things as he suffered to happen to us, if we follow and serve him. He said, 'Blessed are you when people insult you, persecute you and falsely say all kinds of evil against you because of me. Rejoice and be glad, because great is your reward in heaven, for in the same way they persecuted the prophets who were before you' (Matt. 5:11–12).

Those weeks took me deeper in my faith. I trust God, and know that this is his work I am doing, and it will not be destroyed. We have had numerous words and prophecies from God about the hospital we have been called to design and build. No one can stand against him.

But 'the father of lies' (John 8:44) leads people to initiate these negative events as his attacks and 'ammunition' in this spiritual war, to try to create fear and confusion as well as to divide people. The battlefields for the spiritual war we all see evidence of in this world are the hearts and mind of humans; from the governing powers at a strategic level, right down to individual families and personal relationships. This kind of battle has to be fought on our knees.

Most Christians who push forward for God's kingdom, sharing the message of Jesus, fighting against poverty, slavery, abuse, injustice or any of the other dark things in this world, will sooner or later face some kind of attack. For each of us it looks different, but there are often similar hallmarks, and it is something we should expect as part of our journey, and most importantly we shouldn't be put off by them.

The spiritual war is fierce, and it is essential that we surround ourselves in prayer, worship, fellowship with other faithful followers of Christ, as well as immersing ourselves in God's Word as our guide. Our relationship with our Father God, and time spent in his presence, in an attitude of listening, obedience, and worship, is our strength. Spiritual attacks can take so many different forms, whether physical persecution, verbal abuse or defamation, ill health or injury, breakdown of relationships with family, friends, or in a working environment, or in some parts of the world even imprisonment, torture and execution from the community or the authorities.

I remembered a talk that our vicar gave a few years before in which he said that whatever tough or difficult situation we face in our lives, we should ask ourselves what God wants us to learn from the experience. There is always something to learn. We should not suffer in vain.

One thing on my heart was about how we are drawn to pray

in times of trouble. If we are facing persecution, our first instinct is to pray for it to stop. And if we are facing a dangerous situation, our natural intuition is to pray for protection. But the account from Acts 4 had left a big impression on me a few years earlier. For healing a crippled man and preaching the gospel, Peter and John had been arrested, put in prison and questioned by the religious authorities, then warned against preaching about Jesus. After Jesus had been crucified, and with the believers facing these threats, it was clear they were in a time of great persecution. When Peter and John were released and went to the other believers, their prayers surprised and inspired me. It didn't say that they prayed for protection, for safety or for their persecutors to stop, it said they prayed for boldness. Courage to keep preaching, and bravery to keep pushing forward was their priority.

In the end I felt such a strong sense of privilege that God would count me worthy to suffer for serving in his name. I was so close to him in this time, and felt so blessed that he was kind enough to warn me beforehand, and to reassure me in the middle of it. It refined my faith. There was a day when I talked with one of our partners who encouraged me, talking about us and our faith being like gold refined by fire. A couple of hours later one of our faithful prayer warriors sent a message to our prayer group saying that she had been given a picture while praying a few nights before. She said that my work was like gold: eternal and solid. When placed in the refiner's fire, these schemes and slander which try to cover it turn to ash and are blown away. Only the gold remains, and shines brighter. I was encouraged to see and hear this from two people on the same day. The next morning I prayed before taking the children to school, then randomly opened the Bible at Malachi 3:3, which said, 'He will sit as a refiner and purifier of silver; he will purify the Levites and refine them like gold and silver. Then the LORD will have men who will bring offerings in righteousness.'

Something God also put on my heart at this time was the importance of our attitude towards our enemies. Until this point in my life, I had never known anyone that I could have considered an enemy. The concept of not just forgiving but *loving* our enemies was theoretical, rather than something I had ever had the opportunity to put into practice. In the same way Jesus forgave those who scorned him and crucified him, we need to forgive those who try to harm us. Jesus loves them and died as much for them as he did for you and me. Through the love that God poured on Saul, one of the most vigorous persecutors of early Christians was transformed into a dedicated servant of God willing to give his freedom and eventually his life for Jesus. We can't know the future for anyone who works against us or tries to harm us. I chose to forgive my new enemies, and to pray that they would know God's love, mercy and abundant grace and blessings in their lives.

25

The Narrow Road

2019

People sometimes ask whether I am in any danger when I am in Syria. My reply is usually rather functional. I might talk about the bombs and shooting I have seen and heard, about the statistics, and about God's promise to protect me there. But it is in reality a fascinating question.

I have only ever gone to Syria on God's mission, at his instruction, from his provision, and to do his work. I have gone with his promise, so what could be unsafe? I could be in the most dangerous war zone in the world, but if I am there through God's will, then my soul must surely be in the safest place. Can I say I have faith in God if I am unwilling to live that faith, in practice, day by day?

Faith is not an ideological concept that we just believe in our hearts. Nor is it something made real through discussions or debating with other people. It is a way of life we must live out, every day. Faith is only evidenced by actions.

If God is the master and creator of the universe, then can't we trust him with our lives? He holds so much more in his hands. He holds eternity! He knows and made every hair on our heads, and we are precious to him. If he has the ability to design and implement all the laws of science and nature, creating every species on this planet, then we should be willing to take some risks if we are sure we are responding to his calling.

I'm not talking about deliberately and wantonly putting ourselves in danger just for the sake of it. But if we are doing what God asks us to do, in the place he wants us to do it, and if we are listening and responding to him, then he can take care of us there. In the bigger picture, sometimes people suffer or die in the process of serving God, but as a Christian I believe death is not the end, but rather just the beginning, and if we die serving him, then in the end we will gain more than we lose. We will all die one day, and I would rather die serving God's purposes than of a heart attack, stroke, or dementia. Not everyone feels called to die for God, but if we do not trust God, and if we are unwilling to entrust the lives he gave us into his hands, what kind of faith is it we possess? It is not a mature faith. It is the ticket for a journey, but it is a journey we have not yet started.

My dangerous place might be Syria. Your dangerous place might look completely different. Perhaps it is a place in your neighbourhood or city, or visiting someone you have some problems with. Perhaps it is taking a step in your life which feels like a risk, or perhaps you could lose something if it doesn't turn out the way you hope, or you are concerned about your image in someone else's eyes. Maybe it is an important conversation God wants you to have with someone, but you need courage to start it, or the ability to forgive someone who has hurt you.

But if stepping into our dangerous place is doing something which serves God's will, responding to his calling to use our lives to serve him, to serve the poorest, the oppressed, the marginalised, the downtrodden or the vulnerable, or to be a voice for those who have no voice, then everything that happens from there on in is part of the journey he has planned for us, and wants us to experience. Even to death. If Jesus gave his life for us, how many of us are willing to give ours for his sake? This doesn't mean we shouldn't be careful if faced with danger, but rather that we need to weigh prayerfully whether he wants us to be there in the middle of the fire, in the process becoming like gold made pure by the refiner's fire. Facing unimaginable hardships can be part of the journey that will develop our spiritual life.

If we step out in faith to serve him and follow through with what he has called us to, then one of two things will happen: either he will protect us, keeping us safe from harm, or he will allow things to happen to us along the way which are scary or dangerous, but which are part of our life journey. These difficult incidents are character and faith building. Sometimes events take place that are terrifying or painful, but these are the same trials that develop who we are. They are the fire that refines our inner metal. These events equip us to be more in the future than we are today.

Every day we are given is an opportunity, and if every day gives us a fresh chance to do something new or achieve something better, what will we do today? The saddest part would be if we aren't willing to begin that journey in the first place – the journey God has planned for us if we are only willing to trust and step out in faith. It would be tragic if we were, instead, held back by fear: fear of failure, fear of harm, or fear of looking stupid.

The most dangerous place would be to reach the end of our lives without having lived the life God called us to live, without having done the things he asked us to do, or without having loved the way he called us to love. We only get one chance at this life; I don't seek to preserve mine, but instead I seek to live it faithfully and fruitfully. I aim to live it God's way, and trust he will protect it along the road, or take it if he wants me back.

If we have true faith, it will carry us through the roughest and darkest places, no matter how awful they look from the outside. Sometimes from the inside they become the most beautiful places, because it is in them that we are closest to God, and can truly feel him walking and talking with us. He gives us his courage to face every obstacle, every hurdle and every challenge when we reach them, not before. We will certainly face many of these as we walk his narrow and difficult road. They are like signposts showing we are headed in the right direction. They are part of our journey, and the problem any of us is facing right now might just be the greatest opportunity we have ever been given in our lives.

So often we find ourselves at a crossroads. Some decisions are easy to make while others are harder and involve making a choice between taking a straightforward path or walking a road which is narrow, difficult and full of challenges. Working in Syria falls into the second category, without any shadow of a doubt!

There has been nothing easy about working in Syria. From the first moment of wanting to send a large consignment of aid there, to taking nearly two years to eventually find a safe and legal route to send containers into the country, through to the time of writing this book, so many struggles have emerged along the road, and our catalogue of trials grows longer by the day. We have had to become persistent advocates for humble and prayerful problem solving, searching for guidance, and anticipating and preparing for the issues that will present themselves along the way. Sometimes we simply have to offer up situations in prayer and just trust God to work them out.

A war zone is one of the most complex places in which to work. Checkpoints; authorisations; lack of trust; corruption; greed; the breakdown of law and order; the need for armed protection in some places; intelligence agencies and the concerns they have both in the UK as well as in Syria; sanctions; lack of resources; being caught up in fighting; kidnapping; doctors and other male workers suddenly being conscripted into the military; terrorism; criminal gangs trying to intercept aid or extort money; armed militias. Even trying to remain neutral in a war zone causes problems, as both sides will be suspicious of you if you aren't seen to be taking their side. These are just a few of the many challenges and complications we face each week. Syria is so complicated because of the political tensions which exist between the nations and entities that have supported the various factions fighting in this war. The amount of emotionally charged propaganda has stirred up strong and polarised attitudes on each side.

Sometimes people tell me they want to do something like this, working on the front line. But I don't always feel their interest is born out of a deep love for these people; rather, it comes from a hunger for action or excitement. Most people have no idea how their presence could cause enormous problems with one wrong move or statement, however innocent and pure their motivation. I am still learning after a few years spent working daily with our teams on the ground. Such people also have no idea how naïve they are about the real situation in Syria. Naivety can be so dangerous in a place like that – for outsiders, but even more so for the Syrians they are associated with.

Each of the governments involved in the process of providing aid into Syria add challenges to the process. The sanctions imposed against Syria, on paper at least, allow humanitarian aid; the reality, however, is much more complex.

You can send physical aid into Syria, but only certain things from certain places. If you do send aid, you cannot cover the costs to distribute it unless you jump through a multitude of hoops – which can take many months – to gain an authorisation to enable money to be sent which will be spent on buying fuel. Even paying a haulier in Syria counts as buying fuel, and the number of questions asked by our government over weeks and months just to gain an authorisation or to change details on these documents is extreme. We have always worked legally, but it can be exhausting.

Equally, the sanctions imposed on sending finance to Syria have made it extremely difficult for NGOs to get money into the country for humanitarian aid. It has taken an amazing amount of patience and persistence, and continues to require an enormous commitment.

We can use a system for many months, then suddenly, the next time we try it, find that the door has closed, and we have to find a new one, which can take many months. There is no warning when this happens. On one day I may be allowed access into an extremely sensitive centre for displaced people in Syria that includes ex-fighters, then two days later I may be refused entry to a less sensitive centre. After being allowed to visit Syria on three occasions during some of the most tense parts of the conflict, I was then refused entry at the border the fourth time. We resolved it, but it took a month. After sending sixty-three containers of aid and eleven ambulances into Syria, out of the blue we were suddenly told to stop. While we usually resolve all issues in the end, we are often left dangling without an adequate explanation. Finding solutions can take a long time, and it can be so frustrating as we could achieve so much more to serve the people if these processes were more consistent.

Working in a troubled place with shattered trust and fragmented law and order has brought many other challenges. Some people have been suspicious of anyone genuinely helping people free of charge. In Syria we have found few partnerships offered to us which expected nothing in return. Our team has been offered free land to assist the work, only to investigate it further and find it riddled with legal issues and taxes for which they would have become liable had they accepted it. Other offers have been made by people trying to use our work to whitewash their reputation or even use it as a means to enable them to access other connections or advantages.

On one occasion I went with some people from our team to visit some families in Syria who were apparently being supported by one of the churches in Syria. At the end of the visits, the church representative propositioned my Syrian colleague with an arrangement, in which he offered to give a list of names and details of people, in return for them bringing money supposedly to support these families in need. He said that if our team on the ground brought the money to their church, he would give a percentage back to our team member, for them to keep for themselves. He then named some other NGOs that he alleged they already had this arrangement with. I was aware that these kind of practices take place on a significant scale, but was so disappointed to see a church involved in this kind of deceit.

Even providing free medical services to the poorest people caused us problems in one area, as local doctors were unhappy, feeling we were taking their patients. When our teams work honestly with careful attention to detail, refusing to compromise on the ethics of our work, it stirs up contempt from those who are not working in the same way, because it exposes their corruption and dishonesty. Doing the work of Jesus comes at a high price.

Our team and work also becomes visible to dangerous individuals and groups. The Syrian crisis has attracted the attention of people who have a fascination with war or who want to send support to certain groups of fighters, or politically motivated groups, and we have had to avoid these people who have tried to use us as a conduit to support these kind of groups. But we have been more concerned about the charities in the UK that have undoubtedly been assisting jihadists, whether directly or indirectly, wittingly or unwittingly. Most westerners have little or no understanding of the complexities of the Syrian war in spite of what they may have read about it; of who is doing what and where, of why there is a war in the first place, or of who is involved. I have also been contacted by people in the UK with connections to proscribed terrorist organisations, who wanted to form partnerships or get involved in our work. We have needed to use a great deal of prayerful discernment, and for this it has been essential to listen to God in the many different ways he has spoken to us.

Over time we have seen the importance of being more discreet about what we share publicly, including stepping back from social media. Even in areas where terrorist groups were not operating, there have been problems with criminals using sly ways to attempt to blackmail and extort money from people. Humanitarian aid has become a very profitable, multi-million dollar business in Syria during the conflict, and many working in this sector have become rich from their involvement. Some would go to great lengths to get a piece of the prize.

Having worked alongside a number of other NGOs in Syria, as time passed we felt that our mission was not simply to link in with and work in the same way as many humanitarian organisations there. We felt God was calling us to work in a different way, according to his direction. As a result, we only engage with a few other NGOs there. It is safer for our work and for our teams to choose who we work with very carefully.

But we have also found that when we are willing to put ourselves aside, serving God and his agenda, those who are poor and vulnerable, and choosing the narrow road, he guides us, directs us and encourages us so closely through the difficult parts of the journey.

Jesus told us that it is the narrow road that leads to eternal life, and there are few who ever find it. Most choose the wide and easy road. But how far along the narrow and difficult road should we go to help someone else in need? At what point do we judge a situation to be someone else's problem and not ours? Should we say we will serve God, or help our neighbour, and then draw a boundary, geographical or psychological, which puts them outside our definition of neighbour or of what we feel comfortable doing to serve God? At what stage do we say someone is too far away for us to help, or that we would risk too much in trying?

When we choose the easy road, nothing in this world ever changes. Circumstances only change when people are willing to see and feel the pain of others, put themselves out, make difficult choices, get their hands dirty, persevere, take risks which might cost them something – or everything – or sacrifice their comfort in exchange for bringing comfort to someone else who is hurting. But the narrow and difficult road leads to change; it is the road demonstrating true love when we walk it, and it is the road which allows us to grow and develop. When we walk it we learn what it really means to trust God, and he stretches and deepens our faith. This is a true and beautiful faith, like that gold refined by fire.

We may feel we can't change the world. But we can change our own little world, and we can change the world for someone, somewhere, when we are willing to travel further than most on the narrow and difficult road. The more people who are willing to change their own world for the sake of the most vulnerable, and according to God's will, the more good we will see in this life. I always said when I first set out on this journey that if all my efforts and work save the life of just one child, or one person, then *all* my efforts will have been worthwhile.

Every day we have a decision to make about whether we stand side by side with the people suffering in this world, as one voice, and as one body. We have a choice as to whether to avert our eyes and live a more comfortable existence because it is easier, just taking care of our own immediate friends and family, or whether to walk the narrow and difficult road. We have a choice as to whether we will give our lives to serving God.

We should be discerning, though, to be sure when we start to fight a cause that we truly understand who and what we are fighting for. Jesus told us to be 'as wise as serpents and innocent as doves' (Matt. 10:16 ESV), and he also said, 'Your eye is the lamp of your body. When your eyes are healthy, your whole body also is full of light. But when they are unhealthy, your body also is full of darkness. See to it, then, that the light within you is not darkness' (Luke 11:34–36). We live in a world where deception and lies are part of the fabric of our culture. It is hard to escape them. So many lies have been told about the Syrian conflict, as well as about the faithful servants of God. We should seek God's discernment, outside of our own understanding and beyond the information presented to us by the world.

I do not put my faith in governments, and I have very little interest in politics. The governments and the political, religious and ideological movements party to the Syrian war, whether covertly or openly, all have much to answer for. They all have blood on their hands. My faith is in the government of Jesus. God's is the only true and timeless authority, and his kingdom is eternal. We are called to live by and honour the rules of our governments here on earth, providing they do not contradict God's laws to love him, and to love our neighbours. But governments come and go, nations are built and devasted, and empires rise and fall. The one and only thing which remains constant is the living God, who is, who was and who is to come.

The important thing to understand about the narrow and difficult road is that it is a journey. We walk it one step at a time. If you can only manage small steps, then just take those little steps, one at a time. A small step for one of us is a huge step for another. We each have different personal challenges and should never judge others against ourselves. No matter how big or small our steps are, they are all important. But change will only happen when we are willing to leave our comfort zones and start walking.

It's worth taking these little steps to begin, because starting gives you the courage to go further, and build endurance. When someone first starts to exercise, using muscles they are not used to using, it is painful. Parts of the muscles tear and the process hurts. However, the torn muscles start to knit themselves back together, and the newly formed repairs are stronger than the original muscle. This is how we develop our fitness, ability and stamina. The same is true of giving and taking action to make a difference in this world, as well as of walking by faith to serve God. You can never know where it will lead you, but it will certainly be the most exciting and rewarding journey of your life.

26

The Human Condition and the
Kingdom Here on Earth

I have not always had faith. In my early years, I was fascinated by the idea of church, and asked my mother to take me, but she wasn't keen. She married my stepfather when I was eight, and then we started going to a Spirit-filled church in London which I loved, and which laid an important foundation in my relation-ship with God. My mother and stepfather separated when I was a teenager, and I soon lost my faith during those turbulent years. In my early twenties, I settled, but began to feel there was some-thing missing in my life. After my mother, who had by then become a Christian, lent me a book about people who had done the Alpha course, I soon realised it was God I was missing. I then did an Alpha course myself, and asked Jesus into my heart.

There were things I loved about the church I was going to then, and others I struggled with. Eventually I drifted away from the church, and consequently drifted away from God. Years later, after my second child was born, I felt God touch my heart. It was as if he snapped his fingers and suddenly said, 'Samara, it's time now. I want you.' I suddenly felt an urge to read some Christian books, and also picked up the Bible for the first time in years. As I read Matthew's Gospel, I wept when I realised how far I had strayed, and that my life looked so unlike the life Jesus called us all to live.

Realising how important it is to be part of a church, and how hard it is to live as a Christian without a community of believers around you, I found my church, St Peter's, Brighton, which has felt like home ever since. When I walked in for the first time, I saw four huge polystyrene letters in the hall which spelt out LOVE, and I felt my heart jump as I realised that this really is the centre of God's heart, and the Christian message. This was the introduction to my journey in faith, which only really started in earnest as I started to walk the call that God put on my life: to serve him and his kingdom, to love the poor, to care for the sick and to reach out to those in need.

Many times, I have asked myself why God used me to do all these things, why he answered so many of my prayers, and why he has given us such extraordinary guidance. I think the answer is simply because I put myself aside and asked him what I could do to serve him. I asked him to use me in whatever way he saw fit, no matter what the cost. It wasn't about achieving something I wanted: it was about achieving something he wanted. It was never about doing something for myself, or my family; it was about doing something for him, and his family. It was never about building something for my life; it was always about building for others and for his kingdom. I made many sacrifices, choosing to focus on his work rather than on the many things I used to do with my time – spending time with friends, organising holidays and dinners and pleasure-seeking. My prayers since starting this work were not for my own gain; they were prayers for his gain, and for the benefit of those who are poor, vulnerable and lost. Jesus' heart is for people who are poor and broken, and for love, justice, mercy and compassion. When those things become our core, our heart and our reason for living, then his heart and ours begin to beat in the same rhythm.

But I'm not perfect. I'm not a perfect mother or wife. Nor am I a perfect daughter, sister or friend. I make mistakes every day. I am full of shortcomings and, no matter how hard I try, I fail to be what I aspire to be. Maybe I say the wrong thing or forget to do the right thing. Perhaps I overlook something important, or fear or impatience get in the way of making the right decisions. I have this frustrating condition: I am human.

Sometimes I reflect back over the last few years, and how I got here. When I think back to where I was in life when I started this work in August 2014, I wonder who would have looked at me then and chosen me as the suitable person for this.

I was a stay-at-home mum with two little children aged four

and one. I had no experience in charity work, fundraising or project management, and I wouldn't have believed I could take on something which would grow so big so quickly. At that time, I had almost no ability to travel, as I had two young children. I would not have identified myself as someone who could go to a dangerous war zone like Syria. I didn't have a big network of contacts, and I had no experience of public speaking at that time.

It is encouraging to know God does not see us as we see ourselves, or even the way others see us. He doesn't judge us the way we judge each other. Instead, he searches our hearts. His concern is with how we look on the inside, not the outside. He cares about our motivation, about our willingness to start working for his kingdom and to persevere, and about our relationship with him. Our hunger needs to be to serve and give, not to be served or receive.

When God looks at us, he doesn't focus on our weaknesses. If we make him our focus, he doesn't criticise or berate us about failing to live up to what he would like us to be. Nor does he overlook us because we don't have the right skills or experience. He looks past these things and sees our potential. If we are willing to offer the little we do have, he gives us responsibility, leading us step by step, pushing us to our maximum capacity each time, but never giving us more than we can cope with.

He sees us as more than a collection of appearances, words and abilities. The weaker and more humble we are when we give our hearts to him, the more he can do through us. We don't have to be anything special in the world's eyes. He is something special. So we can depend on him to do through us what we are unable to accomplish through our own abilities, or lack of them, providing we are first willing to give everything we have. *Unconditionally.*

I feel this immense gratitude that the master and creator of the universe could look at tiny me and think, 'I can do something through her.' Wow. Little me?

How could I have known he would take ordinary me and give me the opportunity to step out in faith? Or that my tiny steps in the beginning sending clothes from our own wardrobes would lead me to work with so many amazing people, sending more than one million kilograms of aid to the Middle East, providing four field hospitals in Syria, at different times, and sending eleven ambulances, as well as a huge collection of hygiene items and thousands of care packs for pregnant women and babies? How could I have known he would give us a vision to design and build a $35 million plus hospital in one of the most devastated countries in the world?

What wonderful grace he has, to look past all my inadequacies and still decide to use me to make a difference in this world. He doesn't require perfection from any of us, he just requires our willing hearts. Hearts which say, 'I have nothing to give, but the little I have, I will give it all to you.' Hearts which say, 'I can't do it, but everything I can do, I will do it for you.' Hearts which say, 'I am nothing special, but if you are willing to use me in spite of all my failings, I will do anything you ask.'

Nor do we need to wait until we are at the right time and place to get started. It may never come. The call on our lives is right now. Just as we are. Warts and all. This is not a dress rehearsal, this is it. This is our life, here and now. This is our big opportunity. If we wait, we may never get started. We will never be perfect enough, holy enough, experienced enough, strong enough or talented enough. We are just ordinary people. But throughout history God has chosen the ordinary, the weak, the unqualified, the unready and the most unlikely people to use as vehicles through which he does the most amazing things. He uses the ordinary to do the extraordinary.

God's grace is special. It is because of this that he gave the most precious thing he could. He gave his Son Jesus Christ, who willingly went to the most savage and barbaric death to take the punishment for everything wrong we ever did or will do in the future. He paid the price we should have paid, so that we can live in freedom, and spend eternity in paradise with him, if we choose to accept him.

I am thankful for his forgiveness, because I need it every day. I am humbled by his amazing grace, because without it I would have no hope. I am grateful for his mercy, because with him we have the chance to be more than we can be on our own. I am overwhelmed by his unconditional love, because we all need love. We need to give this love as much as we need to receive it.

Before I had children, I did many exciting things in my life. I travelled to exotic countries in Asia and the Caribbean, staying in luxurious hotels. I went snowboarding, scuba diving, wakeboarding, dog sledding. I dined in some of the most exquisite restaurants, visited some of the most prestigious health spas, and more. But these things were superficial, and since I have had a personal relationship with Jesus, they have lost any meaning to me. How can I find any sense of satisfaction in my heart eating a Michelin-starred meal while a child in Africa is starving to death? How could I choose an expensive hotel, knowing a displaced family with small children in Iraq only has a leaking tent to shelter in over winter, with no heating, through driving snow and winds? How can I find any sense of peace in my heart, pampering myself in a luxurious spa while a father of young children in Syria dies of a heart attack because none of the hospitals in his area can treat him?

A number of years ago I picked up a copy of the Bible for the first time in many years. I started reading the Gospels again, curious to remind myself of the teachings of Jesus. It had been a long time. I had felt a little restless, that there was something missing in my life. I had had a lot of fun, but nothing truly hit the spot. The pleasure from those superficial things didn't last long. I soon found myself wanting to start planning the next trip, party or experience.

There are few people who wouldn't agree with the teachings of Jesus: love, forgiveness, sharing, respect, treating others as we want to be treated, caring for the sick, being a voice for the most vulnerable. At that time I thought I was a good person. I was a nurse and always helped my friends and family. But as I read the words of Jesus, my heart sank as I realised my life looked so different from the way he asks us to live. His teachings were radical and are still radical today. I knew he was right, yet I fell short of his example, and still do.

I have been humbled by the patience God has shown me when I have made the wrong choices, when I have ignored someone's needs, when I have been unfaithful to him and his instructions, and when I have let self-indulgence come before serving others in need. Everything God asks of us is something which benefits us in the end, but often we are too stubborn or proud to see it or admit it.

We have tough choices to make. Do we give in to the entitled, consumer-driven, materialistic society we are surrounded by, encouraging us to want more, deserve more, treat ourselves, and feel that 'we are worth it'? Or do we choose his way? Every day we have to make this choice. It is an active decision.

The children starving in Africa deserve to eat three meals every day – as much as my children do. The displaced Iraqi family who are trying to survive in a tent with holes in it through a freezing winter deserve a warm home in winter – as much as my family do. The father having a heart attack in Syria deserves life-saving treatment for his condition – just as we would feel entitled to have it here in the UK.

Perhaps you don't feel you have much, if anything, to give. When we have nothing else to give, we can give the most precious gifts of all: our hearts, and our lives. We can get on our knees, with nothing else to offer but ourselves. When we are willing to give the tiny little we have, however small, and sacrifice our little piece of time, energy, money, belongings and passion, this is where it starts. God sees everything we do, and knows how easy or difficult it is for us. He sees when we feel we have nothing to give, so give our hearts to serve him without reservation. He honours our sacrifices and makes them more than they can be without him.

One thing I have learnt over the last few years is that it really is better to give than to receive. There is no experience we can create or buy which compares with the satisfaction of giving up something we might have liked or wanted, to make a difference instead in the life of someone in great need. We all have something to give, big or small.

If you are searching for something which satisfies more than the short-lived enjoyment gained from material things, or from pleasure-seeking, be sure that Jesus satisfies.

It breaks his heart to see what we, the human race, have done in places like Syria. Yet we have serious problems here in the West too, even if they look different on the surface. The problems we have seen in Syria, many of which have been created or exacerbated by external entities as well as in the West, are the result of a humanity which has rejected the one true God of love, and has instead chosen its own way, feeling it knows best. All the suffering we have seen there has been created by the greed, power struggles and terrible mistakes of humans across the world. The Bible tells us that God will allow these events to take place for a short time, but not for ever. A time is coming when we humans will have to answer for our mistakes, for the things we did which we shouldn't have done, and for the things we didn't do which we should have done.

But God will meet you wherever you are, if you invite him into your heart. He will not meet you in judgement. He comes to you as a poor and humble servant, Jesus Christ, who was willing to wash the feet of his disciples, sacrificing everything, including his dignity and his throne in heaven, to come and live among the likes of us. He was willing to suffer the most painful, ugly and humiliating death to make it possible to meet you exactly where you are, with your big and small mistakes, to wipe your slate clean, and prove to you how precious you are to him.

When we fully open our hearts and surrender to him, we discover a love and peace which go beyond all measure. If we put aside our pride and self-interest, he will take us on a life-changing journey, giving us a new perspective. This journey has been more exciting than any of the superficial things I filled my life with previously. It has been more satisfying than any other experience I had. My relationship with Jesus is more rewarding than any material thing I have ever possessed, or than anything I ever thought I needed. He colours our lives and shows us what true love looks like.

If you lack direction or a true sense of purpose, there is

nothing that can help you find it without true love. But real love is not just a gushy emotion we feel. God is love, and that true love of his is expressed through his ultimate sacrifice for us, in Jesus. Jesus is the only thing that can satisfy us fully, today, tomorrow and for eternity. His death and resurrection is the only thing that can atone for our mistakes, if we realise our need for forgiveness and accept this sacrifice he made for us.

If you haven't done already, you can ask him into your life. He is ready and waiting for you, and he loves you, just as you are. It is simple to humble yourself, say sorry and receive forgiveness for everything you have done wrong and for the right things you haven't done, to thank him for paying the price for your mistakes and invite him into your heart. Unlike people, he will never let you down. He paid the price for your life with his blood. That is real and lasting commitment. This is what *true* love looks like.

Love is not just a noun, it is also a verb: a doing word. It requires action. Jesus has taken the ultimate action on our behalf, in love. Now, we are called to act, in love and compassion, and this is our call to action.

We are all on a journey through this life, and we each have so much to learn. Our mistakes are part of life and we will continue to make them, but we can learn from them, and if we ask God's Holy Spirit to live in our hearts, we can be better today than we were yesterday.

Now, a new phase in my journey begins – to design and build a hospital. Once again, I am stepping out in faith, walking and trusting God to open every door at the right time, and to provide everything we need: the team, the architects, the builders, the doctors, the nurses, the suppliers, and, of course, the money. If this is his project, he will bring each of the right people at the right time, speaking to their hearts, and stirring up their compassion.

The feeling in my heart is that this hospital will be another mosaic. I have a vision of there being many donors, each giving their pieces. Each person will bring a different size, another shape, a distinctive colour, but each piece is essential in the overall finished picture. My vision is of the most light-filled, stunning and beautiful of all the mosaics we have yet made.

We were inspired by the book of Nehemiah, in which the exiled Israelites returned to Jerusalem to rebuild the wall around the city with their own hands. Each family or person took responsibility for different parts, and many heads of the fathers' houses gave financially to the work. Eliashib and his brothers rebuilt the Sheep Gate; the sons of Hassenaah rebuilt the Fish Gate; Joiada and Meshullam repaired the Jeshanah Gate; Malkijah repaired the Tower of the Ovens. Many repaired the section of the wall in front of their house. Like the rebuilding of both the wall and the Temple of Jerusalem, this hospital will be a community effort, for which many people will each take responsibility for a small part.

Our vision is of a radiant hospital which shines light, hope and true love into the lives of many thousands, and also of many thousands around the globe accepting God's invitation to be the artists of this mosaic, and the builders of this hospital. The foundation, every brick, window, door, panel, column, light fitting, screw, bolt, pipe, sink, toilet, bed, sheet, desk, chair, every piece of equipment, and each department – each of these will be the gift of someone, somewhere, towards lighting a lamp of hope for somebody else. Each of these is an essential piece of the bigger picture.

When we add my small amount to your small amount and everyone else's small amount, the results will be breath-taking. When we are willing to give the little we have in our hands, God will multiply our gift, like he did with the two fish and five loaves that were given when Jesus fed the five thousand. Like the few boxes of clothes I had when I started, which were multiplied first to fill a whole lorry, and then to fill over one hundred of these lorries and shipping containers (at the time of writing). Hundreds of thousands of people have now been served through this appeal. In the same way God wanted to share the blessing of giving our possessions with so many here in the UK, I believe he has given us another opportunity to share again, this time through the blessing of being involved in building parts of this hospital of hope, and in so doing, giving the gift of light, hope and life in such a damaged and broken land.

Every step of this journey has been a privilege. Walking the next leg will be the biggest privilege yet. It has been so encouraging walking it with so many beautiful, faithful, caring and generous souls. The people who have walked this journey with me have been such an inspiration and encouragement to me on this road. I am so excited to see what is coming next.

We are called to each do our part to bring good news to the poor, to comfort the broken-hearted, to exchange ashes for beauty, to replace mourning for joyful blessings, and to rebuild the ruins; physical, emotional and spiritual.